Mary
The Imagination of Her Heart

Cowley Publications is a ministry of the brothers of the Society of Saint John the Evangelist, a monastic order in the Episcopal Church. Our mission is to provide books and resources for those seeking spiritual and theological formation. Cowley Publications is committed to developing a new generation of writers and teachers who will encourage people to think and pray in new ways about spirituality, reconciliation, and the future.

❧ Mary ❧
The Imagination of Her Heart

Penelope Duckworth

Cowley Publications
Cambridge, Massachusetts

Published in the United States of America by Cowley Publications, a division of the Society of Saint John the Evangelist. No portion of this book may be reproduced, stored in, or introduced into a retrieval system, or transmitted, in any form or by any means—including photocopying—without the prior written permission of Cowley Publications, except in the case of brief quotations embedded in critical articles and reviews.

Library of Congress Cataloging-in-Publication Data:
Duckworth, Penelope, 1947-
   Mary : the imagination of her heart / Penelope Duckworth.
      p. cm.
   Includes bibliographical references.
   ISBN 1-56101-260-2 (pbk. : alk. paper)
   1. Mary, Blessed Virgin, Saint. I. Title.
BT603.D83 2004
232.91—dc22
                        2004007161

Scripture quotations are taken from *The New Revised Standard Version of the Bible,* Copyright © 1989, by the Division of Christian Education of the National Council of the Churches of Christ in the United States of America. Used by permission.

From "The Manger is Empty." Copyright © 1989 Walter Wangerin, Jr. Used by permission. All rights reserved.

Prayer by Stuart Thomas. Copyright © Stuart Thomas. Used by permission of the author. All rights reserved.

Excerpt from *Family Prayers,* by Nick Aiken and Rowan Williams. Copyright © 2002 Paulist Press, Inc., New York/Mahwah, N.J. Used with permission of Paulist Press. www.paulistpress.com

Cover design: Jennifer Hopcroft
Cover art: "Mother and Child," by Alejandra Vernon. 1999. Used by permission. www.avernon.com

This book was printed in the United States of America on acid-free paper.

Cowley Publications
4 Brattle St.
Cambridge, MA 02138
800-225-1534 • www.cowley.org

For my husband, Dennis,
and our daughter, Clare,
and to honor Mary

Acknowledgments

I am indebted to my husband, Dr. Dennis Gordon, for his abiding support, thoughtful comments, and editorial acumen; and to my sister, Pamela Duckworth Gudish, for help with the manuscript in the early stages. I am also indebted to Cynthia Shattuck, who helped me conceive the book; Vicki Black, who helped critique the proposal; and Kevin Hackett, SSJE, and Michael Wilt, for completing the process with Cowley Publications. I am grateful to Rev. Margaret Schwarzer for help with the initial editing of the book and to Ulrike Guthrie for the patient and skillful editing that brought the book to birth. I am indebted to Rev. Dr. Rosemarie Anderson, Rev. Richard Foster, Samuel Deputy, and Dr. Joseph Grassi for reading and critiquing the manuscript. Others provided support and expertise in their fields, for which I am very grateful. They are the Very Reverend Alan Jones, Rev. Canon Douglas Williams, Dr. Roberta Ervine, the Most Reverend Carlos Touché Porter, Rev. Melitios Webber, Rev. Susan Rodrígues, Rev. Steve Wilson, Rev. Dr. Robert Gregg, Dr. Ebrahim Moosa, Dr. Hester Gelber, Rev. Dr. Ann Winsor, Rev. Phina Borgeson, Nancy Greenfield, Rev. Dr. Gary Brower, Rev. Dr. Arthur Holder, Rev. Portia Mather, Rev. Katherine Lehman, Rev. Leilani Nelson, Dr. Sarah Boss, Rev. Martin Warner, Rev. Beth Hansen, Lydia Lopez, Rev. Marcia Lockwood, Rev. Jeff Millican, Donald Wheland, Rev. Gurdon Brewster, Billie Jean James, Dr. Brigitte Cazelles, Dr. Janet Flammang, Dr. Judith Dunbar, Karen Wallace, Gail Albutt, Rev. Richard Fabian, Betsy Porter, Dan Bradkovich, Dr. Brett Wells, Dr. Harold Perry, and Dr. Jennifer Colby. Cathy Baker, Dr. Georgianna Farren, Anne Hootman, Rebecca Niven, Sarah Peterson, Carolyn Grassi, Dr. Lucretia Mann, and Barbara Ann Long, OP also helped. Any errors in scholarship are entirely my own. I am also grateful for the love and support of my family, especially my daughter, Clare Gordon; my mother, Alice Duckworth; my sister, Claudia Duckworth Dorr; and my great friend Lucy Mack.

I also wish to thank *Theology Today,* in which the poem "Annunciation" first appeared. The poems throughout the book, unless otherwise noted, are all my own.

Table of Contents

1 🐚 Reconsidering Mary

God sent his son, born of a woman. (Galatians 4:4)

MESSENGER

There was an angel at the beginning,
a messenger like a mirror
or a mirage, who shimmered
with the noon and the movements
of her young soul.

There was also an angel at the end,
imposing by the upturned rock
reflecting her stunned silence
then telling her
that blessing drenched and covered
even her astounding losses.

It was the same refracted light but
at first she did not know it:
all she knew was
the brightness shone back
her younger face,
the words echoed
her younger song.

Mary came into my life gradually and through others. Many of my formative years were spent in the South, where Mary was understood simply as a scriptural personage; but as an adult, I have served in an Anglo-Catholic parish that reveres Mary, and I have been influenced by that piety and point of view. During the seventeen years I served as Episcopal Chaplain to Stanford University, people gave me artistic depictions of Mary and books about her. I can't quite pinpoint what spurred my imagination, but as I try to recollect, it may be a copy of the Vladimir icon from Russia that a student brought me from a visit to the Soviet Union in the 1980s. Or it may be a large coffee-table book of the life of Mary, rich with images from Pontormo, Giotto, and Piero Della Francesca, that a visiting professor friend gave me; or a picture of the Madonna of Czestochowa, a dark Madonna with scars on her cheek that the father of a Polish-American bride sent me after I officiated at his daughter's wedding. Each image provoked my curiosity about Mary. Each time a colleague suggested that we study Mary together, each time one of my students asked me to teach him or her the Rosary, Mary's influence on my life was deepened.

As life unfolded, it seemed one image of Mary led to others. A parish gave me a reproduction of a Renaissance Madonna after my daughter was born. A colleague brought me a colorful refrigerator magnet of the Virgin of Guadalupe when he visited New Mexico, and another friend gave me a book on Mary in Mexican culture. Soon I began finding other images on my own. Having images of Mary in my home led me to think more of Mary and to reflect on the various stages of her life—though it led my husband to ask me wryly if the house was becoming a shrine! Actually, I think the images were helping me forge a new understanding and appreciation of Mary. Through those images I was conducting an internal conversation about Mary's role in the biblical story and her role in Christian culture. In the Gospel of Luke, Mary is described as pondering difficult realities in her heart, and through images of her, I was pondering how best to understand her in these times. Although Mary is a preeminent figure in Christianity and one of the most celebrated women in history, to many Christians she seems distant and unapproachable, a porcelain perfection of abstract motherhood that is irrelevant to their day-to-day existence. Within the Episcopal Church and Anglican Communion, historically there have been two perspectives: a "low Church" perspective, in which Mary remains a scriptural and historical personage with little additional recognition; and a "high Church," or Anglo-Catholic point of view, which has revered Mary in various gradations, empowering her by placing her above all other saints and practicing devotions such as the traditional Marian prayers of the Rosary.

Unlike most of the other reformed traditions, the Church of England did not undergo a reversal and devolution in regard to Mary, and the Episcopal Church, along with other members of the Anglican Communion, thus inherited both the Protestant and the Catholic views. Although liturgical change and the common goals of social justice and multiculturalism have downplayed these distinctions in recent decades, the different strains of Marian theology are still played out to some degree in the twenty-first century. Because one or the other of these orientations toward Mary is clearly apparent in other Christian denominations, and because both are being nurtured within the Episcopal Church, which is sometimes called the "bridge church" (being both Catholic and Protestant), a reassessment of Mary from the Episcopal-Anglican tradition will not only serve the Anglican Communion but will have implications for many other Christians as well.

When I began to study what scripture told me about Mary, I realized that what was written could be read in less than half an hour. Yet a computer search of the name *Mary* yields a vast and almost overwhelming array of resources. Mary has been analyzed historically, artistically, culturally, and theologically. Clearly the world does not lack material on Mary. How can we explain this gap between the brief biblical stories and the bottomless well of scholarly, devotional, and cultural material on her? Could it be that the lack of scriptural information has created a relatively pallid image of

Mary compared to the colorful image of Christ, and so gave wider scope to the imagination of the devout? In reality, though Mary has presented a less picturesque canvas on which the faithful could project their longings and needs, the canvas is worthy of study. The images are subtle, and the scriptural colors, though faint, still give us compelling views of Mary that, when explored in depth, yield a more vivid picture. What is revealed is a multidimensional, flesh-and-blood woman—a person no less complex than any contemporary woman. Moreover, the Christian culture over the centuries has added an overlay of its own colors, some of which may need to be judiciously cleared away for a new appreciation to emerge.

In approaching Mary anew, it is important to note that a strange bifurcation exists in our Christian understanding of her that has no parallel in our collective understanding of figures like John the Baptist, Paul, or Peter. Was Mary a perpetual virgin, as some Christians hold, or did she live the life of a wife with Joseph and bear additional children, as other Christians assert? Is she to be revered mainly for her role as mother, or are other dimensions of her life also important to Christian understanding? Questions both long-debated and more recently posed have gained sharper focus in the last century due to momentous events regarding women in the church. In the Episcopal Church (and later in other Anglican Churches), the last twenty-five years have seen the ordination of women to the diaconate, priesthood, and episcopacy, developments that both caused and resulted in a huge upheaval of our understanding of women, women's roles, and women's authority.

Those events also impact our understanding of Mary, and our own relationship to her. For instance, while a priest represents Christ when standing at an altar, a woman priest may also call to mind Christ's mother and the cosmic maternal force some associate with Mary. Changes within the church may challenge our view of Mary and give rise to new questions regarding her place in the institutional church. New insight into dimensions of Mary's identity, brought about by ecclesiastical and cultural changes, calls for a fresh analysis of her. And so, mindful of Mary's identity as woman, wife, and mother, I offer this book from the perspective of a woman, wife, and mother, as well as a poet and priest of the twenty-first century.

Thanks to the vast amount of scholarship, folklore, and religious tradition associated with Mary, and because Mary herself is shown to be a person of many facets, this book is something of a hybrid. It is neither pure theology nor pure history nor pure devotional text, but combines all three, as well as *lectio divina* or meditations on the biblical text. Nor is it linear; it weaves in and out of related subjects, sometimes coming back to them from other angles. This book intentionally situates Mary among other women— women whose stories she would have known from scripture and women she knew as contemporaries. We may assume that she would have been most at home in a community of women, not isolated by her unique calling, because her first action following the Annunciation was to seek out a female confidante.

The book includes poetry and refers to visual art because part of the appeal of Mary has been the art she inspired and continues to inspire. Often Mary first comes to people in images. That was the case historically, when the laity was mostly illiterate and the powerful appeal of certain statues and paintings became legendary, and I believe it is still true today. Mary's story continues to fire the Christian imagination. As a companion exercise to this book, I encourage you to study Mary as she has been celebrated not only in literature and visual art but also in music, theater, and film. The questions for study, reflection, and prayer offered at the end of each chapter can facilitate that process, but I urge you to continue to explore on your own. By engaging the intellect, the heart, and humanity's collective culture, we can better appreciate the fullness of Mary herself.

My personal interest in Mary is shared by many in the Episcopal Church, as is evidenced by church retreats, pilgrimages, liturgical formulations, and church discussions on her. Many are hearing new wisdom in her Magnificat, and are searching for ways to understand her and integrate her into their lives of faith. We inevitably look at Mary from a twenty-first-century perspective, but our appreciation will be deeply enriched if we remember the sources that have influenced our tradition and try to comprehend the grand sweep of Marian devotion in both its ebb and its flow. As the poem at the beginning of this chapter suggests, we will explore the whole life of Mary and seek to comprehend the full circle of her faith. When, from the cross, Jesus entrusted Mary to the disciple he loved and the disciple he loved to his mother, it could be said that he entrusted her to the fledgling church and the church to her. As descendants of that church, we can look to Mary not only as the mother of our Lord but as the mother of a growing, changing church that is finding its way to a contemporary appreciation of her many dimensions, six of which will be addressed in this book. Welcome to this exploration of Mary as prophet, as matriarch, as theologian, as disciple, as intercessor, and as paradigm.

2 🙚 As Prophet

"Greetings, favored one! The Lord is with you." (Luke 1:28)

ANNUNCIATION
(after Fra Angelico at San Marco)

In the ivory colored cloister
acanthus crowns the smooth columns.
Dark arches repeat the ceiling pattern,
the entry shows a small paned window.

Nearby a brown sentry of fence
has not kept out the awesome guest.

He kneels, flush-faced, brimming with purpose;
gold weaves a banner across his chest,
wings tiered amber, jade, carnelian.

She looks past him, her hands protective,
folded across her solar plexus.
In this painting she is not coy
or modest or turned away.

Her face is stark, almost aghast,
and we see soul fight for size.

More is asked than she has got.
It is the moment of summoning up
the language of another future.

We balk and most of us say no;
do not remember being asked.

But he painted and we look
because she saw—beyond the angel—
incipient death, despite the peace
of bell-shaped blossom, greening wood.

She would embrace it all and, yes,
she sent him flying with the news.

ANNUNCIATION

Few scenes have fascinated humankind more than the Annunciation. Artists have depicted Mary's encounter with the angel taking place in drawing rooms and meadows, chapels and bowers. They have shown her giving a variety of responses: She is calm, astounded, terrified, demure. She is seen in the thousands of ways that we see young women and that we see ourselves when we encounter the unexpected divine. Essentially, an annunciation is that moment when a person is confronted with God, when "the Other" speaks to us, enters our world. Several such annunciations are found in the gospels, moments when God's message is announced. They mark those moments when God's plans pull us off course from our own plans.

God continues to announce new directions in our lives, to give us divine messages. Many of us can recall such an encounter. Sometimes we have listened and followed; sometimes we have not. When we have not, we sometimes are given another chance. I remember an encounter that changed my plans. It happened about twelve years ago. My sister had died, and our family had gone back to southern Ohio to put her ashes in an old graveyard on the family farm. I had taken my five-year-old daughter because I wanted her to be part of the memorial service, and I wanted her to meet her great-grandfather, who was then over one hundred years old. He was in a nursing home, and family members said he would not know us.

We had the memorial service, and the next day, on our way out of town, we stopped to see Grandpa. He knew me but was a bit confused about my daughter, and finally said he knew who she was and that she was an angel. He was alert and even humorous, saying he would offer us some of the institutional lunch he had just been served but, speaking as one who had bought livestock feed for decades, he whispered that it was "low grade." We had a pleasant visit, and just as I was about to leave, he mentioned that he would like to go out to the farm. He had not left the nursing home for five years, not since he had broken his hip, and so I nodded and smiled sympathetically, and soon after that we took our leave.

I had not yet reached the door of the nursing home when I was stopped. I don't know what stopped me, but something almost physical let me know that I was not to leave; that I was, rather, to return and take my grandfather out to the farm, the farm he had tended for well over half a century. I telephoned my uncle and discussed it with him, got clearance with the nursing home staff, and then my daughter and I drove Grandpa out to the farm. Despite being a bit confused, he seemed to drink in the place with all its memories.

On the way home, I asked if he would like to stop for an ice cream. We sat in the car at the Dairy Queen while he savored his vanilla alongside his great-granddaughter. When I dropped him off, he looked peaceful and happy. He reiterated that my daughter was an angel, and included me in the category as well. It certainly had been a day of messages, and perhaps real angels had announced a new direction in his life. They clearly had in mine. That was the last time I saw him.

ANNUNCIATION IN THE NEW TESTAMENT

Annunciations happen to many of us, but they happen especially to prophets. God speaks to the prophet, who then speaks on behalf of God. The word *prophet* is believed to come from a lost Hebrew root word meaning "to call" or "to announce."[1] A prophet is therefore generally understood to be one who announces the divine will, or one whose actions demonstrate it. The angel Gabriel announced the divine will to Mary, but it was her action in accepting God's plan that enabled it. The scriptures don't give us much initial information about Mary. What we know is that she was a young woman who heard God's surprising news and accepted her part in it. In the Gospel of Luke, Mary is described as a virgin, and her questions in the story of the Annunciation further verify that. In the Gospel of Matthew, she is described as betrothed. Given the culture of the time and the age of betrothal, most scholars put Mary in her early to mid-teens.

The earliest mention of Mary in the New Testament is in Paul's Epistle to the Galatians, where the apostle tells us that Jesus was "born of a woman, born under the law."[2] From this we know that Jesus' mother was a Jewish woman who observed the religious law. This meant that she worshiped regularly, observed the Sabbath with recited prayers and lighted candles, and followed the dietary and purity laws set forth in Leviticus. We assume that she inherited the cultural understanding of her people: their hopes for a Messiah who would release them from oppression at the hands of the Romans who occupied their land.

The infancy narrative of the Gospel of Luke contains the most information we have about Mary from one gospel source, and it is here that we first hear her voice. Luke sets the stage for the birth of Jesus by the prior announcement of the birth of John the Baptist, and introduces readers to John's parents, the temple priest Zechariah, and his wife, Elizabeth. John the Baptist's birth was announced to Zechariah by the angel Gabriel, but Zechariah did not believe it was possible. He was then struck mute until the birth. Luke contrasts this story with the announcement of the birth of Jesus six months later:

> In the sixth month the angel Gabriel was sent by God to a town in Galilee called Nazareth, to a virgin engaged to a man whose name was Joseph, of the house of David. The virgin's name was Mary. And he came to her and said, "Greetings, favored one! The Lord is with you." But she was much perplexed by his words and pondered what sort of greeting this might be. The angel said to her, "Do not be afraid, Mary, for you have found favor with God. And now, you will conceive in your womb and bear a son, and you will name him Jesus. He will be great, and will be called the Son of the Most High, and the Lord God will give to him the throne of his ancestor David. He will reign over the house of Jacob forever, and of his kingdom there will be no end." Mary said to the angel, "How can this be, since I am a virgin?" The angel said to her, "The Holy Spirit will come upon you, and the power of the Most High will overshadow you; therefore the child to be born will be holy; he will be called Son of God. And now, your relative Elizabeth in her old age has also conceived a son; and this is the sixth month for her who was said to be barren. For nothing will be impossible with God." Then Mary said, "Here am I, the servant of the Lord; let it be with me according to your word." Then the angel departed from her.[3]

The angel Gabriel, who has been described as standing at the left hand of God, is sent to announce both the birth of Jesus and the birth of John the Baptist. Two archangels are named in canonical scripture: Gabriel and Michael. The Greek word *angelo* means "messenger," and a messenger can be in human or nonhuman form. Holy Scripture is full of angels, including the accounts of Abraham and Sarah entertaining them unawares, Jacob's dream of angels climbing a ladder to heaven, the angels singing at Christ's birth, and the angels at the empty tomb. From the earliest days of the church, Christians have had a sense of beneficent and healthful spirits accompanying them. These spirits were often depicted with wings, to symbolize their speed and their travel from another realm to this one.

The angel's news and promise to Mary begins the story of the Incarnation. The name *Jesus*, which the angel announced, is "Joshua" in Hebrew, and links the coming child with his Hebrew forebears, with the throne of David and the house of Jacob. Though Mary's innocence was clearly present in her words "How can this be, since I am a virgin?" she was also pragmatic and knowledgeable about reproduction. She engaged the messenger in conversation, even questioning the archangel, and was no doubt aware of the risks and social stigma involved if she accepted. It is important to note that Mary differed from Elizabeth and other mothers in scripture in that she did not ask for a child. It is also significant that she could have refused to participate in God's plan. Like Abraham had argued before her, she too could have disputed, telling God that this was not the right time and her own situation was too precarious, or that someone else might be better qualified. As the poem at the beginning of this chapter proposes, it is possible that God may have asked others to bear the Christ and they declined. Mary's final response and clear assent made it apparent that she would weigh in on the side of the will of God and not that of personal security or social mores, nor would she disqualify herself for other reasons. Echoing the prophet Isiah's response to God's call, Mary said, "Here am I, the servant of the Lord; let it be with me according to your word." She described herself as a servant of God, one ready to participate in God's great adventure. She did not say, "Let it be with me according to *my* word." Her assent also indicates her inherent confidence and trust in God. She did not question her own qualifications but readily saw herself as a player in the history of salvation. Her assent gives us a clear glimpse of a spiritual and spirited young woman.

The announcement can be interpreted as signaling either a present or a future conception. Views have differed as to whether the announcement corresponded with the moment of conception or whether the conception was yet to come. Indeed, part of the fascination of the Annunciation is the intellectual struggle with the mechanics of the virgin birth. The Greek word for "will come upon you" is *eperchesthai.* New Testament scholar Raymond Brown describes it as "a Lukan verb"; it is used often by Luke and is the same verb used in the Acts of the Apostles to describe the coming of the Holy Spirit at Pentecost. It is not used in a sexual sense. Similarly, the term "will overshadow you" uses the verb *episkiazein,* which describes God's presence in the sanctuary and was used in the gospels for the Transfiguration. Once again there is no evidence for a sexual interpretation.[4]

Although there is no reason for a sexual interpretation, the facts surrounding human reproduction persist as the mind tries to encompass the divine will overriding the nature it established to bring about a new creation. And it is a love story. Properly understood, the Annunciation is analogous to the Christian conversion experience, which is essentially a romance of the soul. God approaches and engages a person with the devotion of a lover, and as we see in the saints (Teresa of Ávila and Francis of Assisi are both excellent examples), lifelong adoration is the appropriate response. The Annunciation teases the imagination to conceive Christ in each life, and the lightness, subtlety, and grace of the event can easily be missed. Mary was the first to struggle with the concept. For Mary to meet the annunciating angel meant that she encountered the transcendence and otherness of God; for her to give her consent meant that she also discovered the immanence of God and found a fresh, radiant, and new possibility for her own life.

Interpretations of the moment of conception have been rich and vivid. A surviving fifteenth-century stained-glass window at the Church of Saint Peter Mancroft, in Norwich, England, shows the infant riding a beam of light and carrying a small cross as the angel announces God's plan to the listening virgin.[5] These lines from Walter Wangerin's contemporary poem "Antistrophe" emphasize Mary's biological participation:

> Then, just then, I felt . . . I call it a "stitching"
> In my right side, low down and deep. Stand! Stand
> Up, Mary, I thought; but I could not move.
> This ache in my pelvis, this light larval spasm—
>
> I, who had never known motion in the caves of
> My womanhood, cried: "The egg . . . drops! Oh, my love!"[6]

THE VIRGIN BIRTH

The virgin birth, which is attested to in both of the major creeds of Christianity, stands as one of the miracles of the New Testament. As with the Resurrection, God is understood to have suspended the order of the natural world and intervened. Contemporary voices, some of which have refuted the virgin birth and others which have reinterpreted it, have enriched our understanding. Bishop John Shelby Spong, who refutes the virgin birth, believes the concept arose naturally as a way of explaining the clear spirituality of the astonishing person of Jesus. John MacQuarrie sees Mary's virginity as giving her dignity independent of her role as wife or mother.[7]

Hans Küng, a Roman Catholic theologian, said: "No one can be obliged to believe in the biological fact of a virginal conception or birth. Christian faith is related—even without a virgin birth—to the crucified and still living Jesus manifested in his unmistakability and underivability."[8] Although the virgin birth is a doctrine that is debated anew in each generation, it nonetheless is clear that Jesus was a person of such heightened and striking spirituality that people saw him as an authority on spiritual issues and would come to him and ask how he had become that way. It seemed he had been born by a different process. An example was the teacher Nicodemus, who came to Jesus and asked how he could be born in the spirit, as Jesus clearly had been.[9] The virgin birth is one means of explanation, and it is helpful to look at the relationship between virginity and spirituality.

Jean Shinoda Bolen, a Jungian psychiatrist, discusses psychological virginity as a person's sufficiency unto herself or himself regardless of sexual experience. In discussing the followers of the virgin goddesses of classical Greece and Rome, she maintains that physical virginity was secondary to an inviolable sense of self, an identity by which a person did not define herself or himself in terms of relationships.[10] By developing such an understanding of self, even victims of rape or abusive sexual relationships might discover within themselves an invincible purity. Such a person is not defeated by damaging relationships. Similarly, a person with no sexual experience who is bound in destructive ways to other people or institutions might be said to have lost her or his capacity for virginity or purity.

If we understand virginity as chastity, and chastity as being emotionally true or as the purity of heart that Jesus spoke of in the Beatitudes, we see another dimension of Mary and her attraction through the centuries. Norman Pittenger suggests that much of her powerful appeal is in her sincerity and her ability to conform her will simply and singularly to the will of God. In his understanding, chastity is not the denial or rejection of human sexuality but the dedicated emotional sincerity of the whole person.[11]

The value of actual physical virginity in our media-driven contemporary culture, which equates human fulfillment with the biological drive for genital activity and views as unnatural or deficient people who are not sexually active, is a huge challenge to the contemporary church, even though we see the disordered and destructive dimensions of sexual license all around. In this era of effective birth control, when the deterrent to sexual expression is no longer unwanted pregnancy and when "safe sex" can minimize the spread of disease, the spiritual potential of sexual intimacy becomes an issue. As Presiding Bishop Frank Griswold writes: "Could it be that one of the freedoms the Spirit of Christ seeks to work in us is the liberation of our sexuality and the capacity to see that it, along with all of God's creative acts, is very good? The answer is yes. However, that which is very good stands in need of discipline and boundaries if it is to bear the fruit of the Spirit."[12]

The wisdom of the church holds that sexual expression best belongs within the context of lifelong commitment to another and to the principle of sacrificing love. The paradox of sexual intimacy is that it can open two people to more than their relationship, inspiring them to reach out to others and show others an image of the love of God. When this occurs physical love has become a sacrament and has fulfilled the expressed hope of Christian marriage. It is an exterior sign of an interior blessing.

THE VISITATION

Immediately following the angel's announcement, Mary went to visit her cousin Elizabeth:

> In those days Mary set out and went with haste to a Judean town in the hill country, where she entered the house of Zechariah and greeted Elizabeth. When Elizabeth heard Mary's greeting, the child leaped in her womb. And Elizabeth was filled with the Holy Spirit and exclaimed with a loud cry, "Blessed are you among women, and blessed is the fruit of your womb. And why has this happened to me, that the mother of my Lord comes to me? For as soon as I heard the sound of your greeting, the child in my womb leaped for joy. And blessed is she who believed that there would be a fulfillment of what was spoken to her by the Lord.[13]

The accounts tell us that Mary went with haste to visit her older cousin who lived in the hill country about fifty miles south of Nazareth. Haste implies excitement and anxiety. After the events she had experienced, Mary needed someone with whom she could find understanding and share her joy, and the news of Elizabeth's pregnancy had told her that Elizabeth was such a person. Her visit to Elizabeth also suggests that she sought out the nurturing and mothering love of an older woman. Her own mother may have died, or Elizabeth may have been one of those people from the older generation who is in tune with youth and able to support a young person who is in crisis, which Mary was.

Clearly Elizabeth had such qualities, because she allowed her son, John the Baptist, to grow into his unusual vocation unencumbered. Perhaps Mary had already spoken with Joseph and seen his hurt and confusion, and even though his feelings were soon replaced with renewed trust, she may have longed for the less complicated support that an older woman and family member could give. Both women had found their respective men folk slow to comprehend the miracles that were engulfing their lives, but suddenly in each other they found someone who could keep pace with their own accelerated understanding.

As sometimes happens, the sharing of faith can give a relationship new depth. When these two women met, there was an explosion of joy, as if unseen worlds had joined forces. This was occasioned when the infant Elizabeth was carrying gave a sudden jump. John the Baptist in utero had signaled his enthusiasm, and suddenly both women shared their excitement that they had been given a part to play in God's plan. Both women carried a part of the salvation of their people. Elizabeth carried a prophet in the ancient mold of the prophets of Israel, and Mary carried a prophet as well, but one who would sing a new song, whose ideas she could almost glimpse. But the jump of John the Baptist also may have been the tiny prophet's recognition of the meeting of two women, both of whom, in different ways, shared his vocation.

In this visit of two pregnant women, one past childbearing years and the other very young, we hear prophetic speeches filled with energy. Elizabeth echoed the words of Deborah celebrating Jael, calling her "most blessed of women" in the Book of Judges.[14] A portion of Elizabeth's words to Mary (along with those of the angel Gabriel) have resonated throughout history because they form the scriptural portion of the words of the traditional Rosary. They are prophetic words because Elizabeth had realized the significance of Mary's pregnancy before Mary told her. Mary's response is also prophetic. In fact, some early manuscripts attribute Mary's response, or the Magnificat, to Elizabeth.[15] Perhaps it is because the prophetic strain is clear in both voices, and so they were conflated into one. It is noteworthy that while Elizabeth's words praise Mary as a woman, Mary turns her words to the praise of God.

THE MAGNIFICAT

The Magnificat (so called because of the opening word in Latin), also called the Song of Mary, echoes the Old Testament words of Hannah[16] when she learned that she would conceive Samuel. It also resounds as a jubilant response, such as Judith gave when women blessed her in the Apocryphal book by her name.[17] And its words prefigure the words of the Beatitudes of Jesus. In the Magnificat Mary's voice joins many voices that challenged Israel, including the prophets Habakkuk, Micah, Isaiah, and Malachi. We also hear in it a refrain from the psalms, particularly Psalm 103, as well as in distant echoes of the Song of Miriam, Mary's namesake, with her joy in God's reversal of the Hebrew plight in Egypt.[18] It is in the spirit of the prophets of the Old Testament, and links their ancient hope with the beginning of its fulfillment:

> My soul magnifies the Lord,
>   and my spirit rejoices in God my Savior,
> for he has looked with favor on the lowliness of his servant.
>   Surely, from now on all generations will call me blessed;
> for the mighty one has done great things for me,
>   and holy is his name.
> His mercy is for those who fear him from generation to generation.
> He has shown strength with his arm;
>   he has scattered the proud in the thoughts of their hearts.
> He has brought down the powerful from their thrones,
>   and lifted up the lowly;
> he has filled the hungry with good things,
>   and sent the rich away empty.
> He has helped his servant Israel,
>   in remembrance of his mercy,
> according to the promise he made to our ancestors,
>   to Abraham and to his descendants forever.[19]

Here we see Mary, the Hebrew maiden living in occupied territory, well aware of the tensions between oppressor and oppressed. Her situation is socially precarious, and ostracism and rejection are real possibilities. She has gone to the home of an established and socially prominent relative. One might expect her to cower before potential criticism, but instead she throws back her head and sings her song, telling how her whole being delights in the will of God. While still a teenager, her entire person enlarges the work of God, and she is emboldened and impassioned in her love for God and for the honor God has bestowed on her. She has become an embodiment of the transforming work of God.

Her understanding of God draws from the rich sources of Hebrew prophecy and poetry, and as her song continues, it is the voice of a prophet, one of those who perceived and proclaimed the divine reality in their midst. Her song is rich in psychological and spiritual understanding. She understood that God desired mercy, and when it was not forthcoming, then through God's action, the proud would be scattered in the imagination of their hearts. They would be confused and unable to conceive of themselves without their usual condition of control. Their confidence would be shattered, there would be a reversal of power, and the poor and lowly would be lifted up; they would find encouragement and support in the imagination of their hearts. She understood God's intent to bring salvation to Israel, and she speaks as the representative of the true Israel. This is indicated in the song when she switches from the first person singular, saying, "The mighty one has done great things for me," to the third person plural, in which she says, "His mercy is for those who fear him."

If we have not bestowed on Mary the title of prophet from God's announcement to her, then the Magnificat would be sufficient to give her that title, in that it fulfills the prophetic purpose as described by Walter Brueggemann in his book *The Prophetic Imagination:* "The task of prophetic ministry is to nurture, nourish, and evoke a consciousness and perception alternative to the consciousness and perception of the dominant culture around us."[20] Mary's song kindles anger at the status quo and hope for a new world to come. Although the Magnificat has been beautifully arranged for choral voices and sung repeatedly in daily offices, it remains a stark challenge to inequity and a call to faith for the dispossessed. Martin Luther said that Mary sang her Magnificat "not for herself alone but for us all, to sing it after her."[21]

The prophet gives language to the often silent voices of those who have a different hope, a different vision, a different dream of the future. The prophetic voice may concern a specific issue, a specific point in time, or it may address the ongoing and enduring situation of human frailty. We should note that the idea of prophecy as prediction has almost disappeared from contemporary scholarship. When Mary delivers the Magnificat, she stands in the line of the prophets, the truth-speakers of Israel who were inspired by the Holy Spirit. It is they who deliver God's word to the people. They interpret history as revealing God's moral sovereignty. Mary's words hearken clear back to Abraham and the promise God made to the patriarch that he would be a blessing.[22] Mary is also called blessed by Elizabeth, who claims that future generations will call her blessed. It is unlikely that the connection between Mary's experience and that of Abraham was lost on either woman. But most important, Mary delivered God's word not only in the words she spoke but also in her physical delivery of the Christ child, who is called the Word Incarnate.

It is significant that while Christianity has been reluctant to name Mary as a prophet, Islam places her closer to that calling. A prophet in Islam is not only someone who speaks God's words but also one to whom God speaks and who listens. Mary (or Maryam) is the only woman named in the Qur'an, and she is greatly esteemed in that religious tradition. Her name is mentioned more often than it is in the New Testament and a section of the Qur'an is named for her. Although Mary is not officially named a prophet in Islam, she is accorded the status of infallibility, a status reserved for prophets, meaning she can err but not sin.

Though the Magnificat is a hymn and a poem, it is foremost prophecy. Rubem A. Alves says the prophet is one who stands empty before the spirit of God. He or she speaks, invoking the holy one, and proclaiming that which will renew the hopes of the dead and challenge the deadness in the living. Prophecy is the place where the artist and the theologian intersect.[23] Seeking ultimate truth and at the same time seeking to utter the divine mystery require that one exercise both the active and the contemplative life. One who would speak prophetically must be not only honest about what is, but also faithful to the source of ultimate reality and willing to suffer to enable the message and methods of that ultimate reality to transform the confusions and contradictions of the times. Speaking truth to power is the work of the prophet, and it is work that continues to shape history. It is neither a popular nor a profitable vocation. Faith-based activism for justice always struggles against the status quo, urging people to alertness to the inequities of the times. Down through the ages, people have found their voices to speak out despite fear, oppression, disapproval, and even official silencing. The realization of God's reign on earth requires that truth continue to be spoken despite the costs.

The idea of a woman prophet was not a foreign one to the Hebrews, even though a woman was not officially allowed to bear witness. Moses' sister, Miriam, had been known as a prophet, and her words are retold in Exodus.[24] It is noteworthy that a prophetic dream before the birth of her brother Moses was attributed to Miriam, who was Mary's namesake. When Miriam reported her dream, her parents did not believe her. The story is told in Jewish writings from the New Testament period.[25] Similarly, Joseph did not believe Mary's story of the Annunciation.

Another prophet, Huldah, is chronicled in the Second Book of Kings,[26] which tells how she wisely perceived the veracity of a scroll of scripture for King Josiah. Deborah, also named a prophet, served as a judge of Israel. The Book of Judges tells how she called Barak to lead the people of Israel to victory over the Canaanites and especially the Canaanites' general, Sisera. Barak held Deborah in such high esteem that he refused to go into battle unless she went with him. As it turned out, the Israelites defeated the Canaanite army, but Sisera escaped and went to the politically neutral tent of Heber the Kenite. Heber's wife, Jael, met Sisera and invited the general inside. She gave him food and invited him to rest, but as he slept, she killed him by driving a tent peg into his temple. Following Sisera's death the Israelites destroyed the king of the Canaanites and were free from their oppression for the next forty years.

Scripture records the Song of Deborah, a celebratory account of the deeds of the Israelite army and a paean to Jael, whom she hailed as "most blessed of women" (a phrase closely repeated in Elizabeth's greeting to Mary). Her song is one of the earliest and most important examples of Hebrew poetry. Near the end of the song, Deborah describes the mother of Sisera:

Out of the window she peered,
    the mother of Sisera gazed through the lattice:
"Why is his chariot so long in coming?
    Why tarry the hoofbeats of his chariots?"
Her wisest ladies make answer,

indeed, she answers the question herself:
"Are they not finding and dividing the spoil?—
    A girl or two for every man;
spoil of dyed stuffs for Sisera,
    spoil of dyed stuffs embroidered,
    two pieces of dyed work embroidered for my neck as spoil?"

So perish all your enemies, O Lord!
    But may your friends be like the sun as it rises in its might.[27]

Despite its literary effectiveness, the bellicosity in the Song of Deborah, as well as the triumphalism that envisions the grief of Sisera's mother, are troubling to most modern sensibilities. The words of the Magnificat have also been viewed as warlike by some, but while God's actions that have "scattered the proud in the thoughts of their hearts," "brought down the powerful from their thrones," and "sent the rich away empty" do imply a clear reversal of the social and political order, they do not necessarily celebrate violence. In this sense the Magnificat differs from the Song of Miriam, which is jubilant over the defeat and death of the Egyptians; the Song of Deborah, which rejoices over the death of Sisera; and even the prayer of Hannah, which says, "My mouth derides my enemies, because I rejoice in my victory."[28]

Mary clearly takes inspiration from the women who preceded her, but her song is a new song. Nevertheless, it is worth noting that the greatest warrior saint in the Christian calendar, Joan of Arc, had a special devotion to Mary, and as a child would often pick wildflowers to make garlands for a statue of Mary in a chapel near her village. When she began her military campaign, she designed her own standard, and her flag carried the names of both Jesus and Mary. Even though medieval France was devoted to Mary, it still is not difficult to see how the Magnificat in particular might have inspired Joan's most unusual confidence and valor.

Mary's words continue to inspire and enrich lives of faith. Rowan Williams, Archbishop of Canterbury, has written a contemporary prayer echoing the Magnificat:

My breath, my heart, my mind,
    my whole life fills with joy
because of God, who's not forgotten me,

whose strength surrounds and lifts me up.
All through the centuries that have passed
   God showed his patience and forgiveness;
God makes the proud and pompous folk look foolish,
   and cares for the simple ones who trust him.
God turns the rich and selfish into beggars.
   God feeds the hungry and the poor.
All through the centuries, God is faithful
   to those he promises will be his friends.
Your beauty fills the earth and the sky;
   the saints and angels sing to you;
God everlasting, Father, Son and Holy Spirit.[29]

MARY'S INFLUENCE ON JESUS

The themes in the Magnificat echo those of the Hebrew prophets, but Mary has composed a unique song, three of whose prophetic themes stand out clearly and are more fully developed in her son. It is interesting to imagine the way in which those themes were inculcated from mother to child. First, she emphasized the mercy of God, the only noun she used twice, and Jesus made mercy a fundamental tenet of his gospel. Not only did he ask mercy of his followers, saying, "Be merciful, just as your Father is merciful"[30] and "Blessed are the merciful, for they will receive mercy,"[31] but he responded to and healed those who asked him to have mercy. He taught mercy in the parable of the unforgiving servant,[32] and his understanding of mercy was clearly based in his relationship with God. This was shown in his response to those who questioned his disciples about Jesus eating with tax collectors and sinners when he quoted the prophet Hosea, "Go and learn what this means, 'I desire mercy, not sacrifice.'"[33]

Second, Mary aligned herself with the poor, and understood God as the God of the poor. Her understanding is that God has "filled the hungry with good things, and sent the rich away empty." She stands in line with the prophet Amos, who railed against those who were "buying the poor for silver and the needy for a pair of sandals."[34] Similarly, when Jesus began his ministry in Nazareth by reading from the prophet Isaiah, he chose the passage that said, "The Spirit of the Lord is upon me, because he has anointed me to bring good news to the poor."[35] In the Beatitudes Jesus contrasted the poor and the rich, as Mary had done: "Blessed are you who are poor, for yours is the kingdom of God. . . . But woe to you who are rich, for you have received your consolation."[36] Jesus lived in poverty, and understood those who lived close to the bone. To choose poverty—then as now—deeply challenged the ways of the world. Jesus knew that possessions could be a block to God, and instructed his disciples to travel with no money or extra clothing.[37] He knew that complete dependence on God nourishes the human spirit, and he included this phrase in the prayer he taught: "Give us each day our daily bread."[38]

The third prophetic theme that Mary brought forward in the Magnificat, and that Jesus amplified, was that God is a God of the humble. She understood that pride had been and continued to be the great weakness of humanity before God, the original sin that drove Adam and Eve to seek to be as gods. The prophet Micah had determined what God required of humanity: "To do justice, and to love kindness, and to walk humbly with your God."[39] Mary described God as having "looked with favor on the lowliness of his servant," and having "lifted up the lowly." Despite the honor she had been given, she maintained a right relationship with God, which Jesus also maintained through the three grueling temptations in the desert. Later on, when Jesus invited the disciples to follow him, he said, "Learn from me; for I am gentle and humble in heart, and you will find rest for your souls."[40] And he instructed his followers not to take a place of honor but to take the lowest place at table, "for all who exalt themselves will be humbled, and those who humble themselves will be exalted."[41]

These themes of the Magnificat are fully realized and clarified in the life of Jesus. A youthful Mary condemns "the powerful" and "the rich," as did the prophets of old, and in this we see the roots of what would become Jesus' teaching. Though we can only speculate on the impact of Mary's prophetic witness on her son, we might also assume that it was because of her influence that Jesus always took women seriously and urged them toward full status in God's reign. No disparaging word toward women is recorded to have passed his lips; rather, he championed women's full potential and viewed them as valued friends, thoughtful conversationalists, and reliable witnesses.

THE WISDOM OF OLDER WOMEN

We are told that Mary stayed with Elizabeth for three months, which was the first trimester of her pregnancy, the time of morning sickness, nausea, possible miscarriage, and weariness. It is when a woman's body adjusts to her pregnancy and, in a sense, assents to its demands. Perhaps Mary needed to be with Elizabeth during that time so that her full physical assent would be supported in the first difficult months. And Elizabeth was in her last trimester, often the most physically trying part of a pregnancy, and she was not a young woman. It is likely that her body ached from bearing the growing weight, and a helpful young companion would have been welcome.

We may assume that Mary stayed until Elizabeth delivered her child. She probably helped with the housework and cared for the infant John the Baptist as Elizabeth regained her strength. She saw what childbirth was like and learned something of mothering an infant. These were probably happy and hopeful times. Neither woman could see what would lie ahead—John's head on a platter borne by a dancing girl and Jesus nailed to a crossbar in agony and disgrace. Nor could they see that future tomb, which would become a womb for unimagined new life. All they could see was their inclusion in the beginning of God's work.

However, Elizabeth's was not the only prophetic voice that Mary encountered. In the Gospel of Luke, when Mary went to the temple to give the offering prescribed in Leviticus, she met with Simeon, who spoke of the destiny of the child and of Mary. His words were a mix of affirmation and warning. He spoke of the child as the awaited savior, but he also warned Mary that a sword would cause her grievous pain. But in addition to Simeon, another prophet—a woman—was there:

> There was also a prophet, Anna, the daughter of Phanuel, of the tribe of Asher. She was of a great age, having lived with her husband seven years after her marriage, then as a widow to the age of eighty-four. She never left the temple but worshiped there with fasting and prayer night and day. At that moment she came,

and began to praise God and to speak about the child to all who were looking for the redemption of Israel.[42]

Anna's heritage as a member of the tribe of Asher is interesting because she represents the northern tribes and exiles. Her tribe lived on the west coast of the Galilean highlands, which had close contact with the maritime city of Tyre and so was seen as having a half-caste standing. Hers was the tribe that sprang from the eighth son of Jacob by Leah's maid, Zilpah. Consequently, of the twelve tribes, it was among those with a lower status. As a member of this tribe, Anna knew lack of social influence; as a woman she knew vulnerability; as a widow she knew loss; and as a prophet she knew God. Her presence at the temple demonstrates that Jesus came to fulfill the messianic hopes of all the tribes of Israel, even the most remote and far flung.[43] Her life as an elderly widow who never left the temple is clarified if we recall that after menopause she would no longer be deemed ritually unclean. And her continuous worship is better understood if we remember the expressed desire at the conclusion of the Twenty-third Psalm, which Isaac Watts paraphrased beautifully: "Oh, may thy house be mine abode and all my works be praise. There would I find a settled rest, while others go and come; no more a stranger or a guest, but like a child at home."[44]

It is important to note that Anna was the very first person to see and proclaim Jesus as the Messiah. She announced to all who were awaiting the liberation of Israel that the deliverer had come. She must have seen in Jesus' tiny face something extraordinary. She must have recognized in him some understanding of vulnerability and loss as well as the news of a triumph that comes of and through it. Unfortunately, the gospels do not record what she said. All we know is that she was present and aware of what was happening. But if we assume that each significant encounter we have influences who we become, then we may assume that Mary's encounter with another woman who was reputed to stand in the line of the prophets shaped the woman she was becoming as well as the man Jesus became. We know Anna was an older woman, like Mary's cousin Elizabeth. Whereas Elizabeth speaks in the gospel, Anna does not. But prophets do speak; that in part is what makes them prophets. This poem explores what Anna might have said:

THE SONG OF ANNA

I stand beside the temple pillar.
    I watch and wait, testing this wonder.
Is the time at last arriving?
    Has Yahweh entered a house of clay?
Only when Simeon whispered the sword,
    I felt unpinned from mortal pain.
A grief was there but six-winged solace
    sang the same tone as the sunlight,
incongruous with the young wife
    holding the recently bartered pigeons,
her husband's eyes fresh from dreaming,
    the gurgling child in ancient arms.
I hum in the shadows, just simple words come,
    I trust the plain words, make this song:

A birthday always has a deathday,
    a sword starts coming down the years,
a birthday always has a deathday,
    reminding us with blood and tears.
A child is here—a sword is coming.
    A child is here—to stop its sting,
a child whose deathday has a birthday,
    a child reversing everything.

No one noted my simple ditty,
    no scribe remembered to pen it down.
Some passersby thought I was senile,
    talking to ghosts among the shadows.
I see the couple stumble their way,
    still absorbing the old man's phrases.
Simeon's eyes are blind with light,
    more than falls between the columns.
I see her offer the flapping doves
    to the priest who blankly sees
the baby's head with wisps of black,
    arms reaching for the bars of light.
It's you, O small one, I make this for,
    I sing you into my bones' red core.

These bones feel deathday in the offing.
    Who knows the morning I will die?
But I don't fear my mortal ending
    for I saw Yahweh in this child's eye:

This child will take the sword that is coming,
this child will suffer, his body break.
I saw death roar proud in his future
but bold life spring up in its wake.

Anna's reputation as a prophet remains despite the scriptural silence. Mary, on closer study, is clearly shown to carry the legacy and moral force of the prophets, even if the title has not been applied to her. It is time that changed. Not only did God announce the divine will to her but she courageously embraced a future that would scandalize the status quo. In addition, she found her own voice to proclaim God's will and its broader implications, and her words have encouraged and emboldened those who recite them through the ages. Her example surely has encouraged others from the church's beginnings, such as the four daughters of Philip the Evangelist, who were known as prophets.[45] In the Magnificat we hear a young woman touch the locus of her power, adding a new and distinct link in the chain of songs of triumph that her foremothers sang, and prefiguring ideas that would find their fullest expression in the Sermon on the Mount and in Jesus himself. The power she unleashes in the song bears fruit in Christ's power to heal, overturn, and resurrect.

THE WEDDING AT CANA

The images of Mary that unfold in the gospels give us glimpses of a complex and evolving person. As Jesus grows, Mary tries to understand this puzzling being with whom she has been entrusted. She is a present but fallible supporter who at times does not understand what Jesus is doing. Because of the frailty of human nature, prophecy, like wisdom, ebbs and flows. Her moment of clarity as represented when she sang the Magnificat becomes only a memory as her days are clouded with the stresses and worries of everyday living. Her other roles take center stage and the wise, prophetic young woman becomes an anxious parent and gradual disciple. But the prophetic imagination has only lain dormant, and three decades later, we see her prophetic witness realized again during the wedding at Cana, when she alone recognizes the fullness of time.

Cana is a village about three miles from Nazareth. Village

weddings were large community celebrations, and the festivities lasted for seven days with fresh guests arriving each day. Food was plentiful and wine flowed freely, and it was understandably difficult to calculate food and drink for guests for seven days. The wedding ritual was ancient and prescribed, and viewed as showing forth again the bond God had made with the Jewish people. People would leave their work, and men would put on a special garment that was worn only at weddings. Jesus and his friends arrived near the end of the week, as the wine supply was running low.

> On the third day there was a wedding in Cana of Galilee, and the mother of Jesus was there. Jesus and his disciples had also been invited to the wedding. When the wine gave out, the mother of Jesus said to him, "They have no wine." And Jesus said to her, "Woman, what concern is that to you and to me? My hour has not yet come," His mother said to the servants, "Do whatever he tells you." Now standing there were six stone water jars for the Jewish rites of purification, each holding twenty or thirty gallons. Jesus said to them, "Fill the jars with water." And they filled them up to the brim. He said to them, "Now draw some out, and take it to the chief steward." So they took it. When the steward tasted the water that had become wine, and did not know where it came from (though the servants who had drawn the water knew), the steward called the bridegroom and said to him, "Everyone serves the good wine first, and then the inferior wine after the guests have become drunk. But you have kept the good wine until now." Jesus did this, the first of his signs, in Cana of Galilee, and revealed his glory; and his disciples believed in him.[46]

Our gospel tells us that Mary was there when Jesus and his disciples arrived. Weddings, then as now, were generally intergenerational gatherings of family and friends. And then as now, it was typically women who organized marriage ceremonies and festivities; such celebrations are often great and consuming events in their lives. In part they are occasions to honor the bride—and the feminine, which a bride represents in the culture—and women invest a great deal of energy in planning and carrying out these events.

Mary was presumably familiar with weddings in the community. The earliest of the gospels tells us that she was a mother of daughters,[47] and as a married woman, she herself had once been a bride. She would have known the emotional and material cost of the event and how important it was to the young couple and the hosting family, which usually would have been the groom's. In this passage we see Mary taking on the role of elder in the community, a wise person, a crone in the positive sense of the word. The failure of the wine supply would be a grave embarrassment to the hosting family and would prematurely end the festivities. It would become a painful memory for the couple as years passed, and any subsequent family failure could potentially set tongues wagging to recall the ill portent at the nuptials. Mary was concerned for the family, and brought it to Jesus' attention. Jesus responded: "Woman, what concern is that to you and to me? My hour has not yet come."

This response has prompted much commentary by biblical scholars, first, because the address of "Woman" sounds harsh and dismissive to modern ears. In fact, it was neither. It is a form of address that was typical of the time and has no negative connotations. But it does emphasize that Jesus did not want his mother to presume any special favor on account of kinship. The connection he sought with his followers was faith and not flesh. His statement "What concern is that to you and to me?" has also puzzled scholars because it is a phrase that is difficult to translate but essentially requests noninvolvement. Then Jesus added by way of explanation for his request, "My hour has not yet come." This too has been puzzling to commentators, and some believe it refers to the hour of Jesus' Passion, but it also could easily refer to his personal timetable for beginning his public ministry. He had to be guided by his own awareness of the right time, and would not be rushed.

Despite resistance Mary proceeded, confident that her son would help, and she directed the servants to do as Jesus told them. "Do whatever he tells you," she said. It is interesting that her words echoed the words of the Pharaoh to the people of Egypt concerning Joseph, "What he says to you, do."[48] Pharaoh's words demonstrated the high regard Joseph had attained. Mary's reiteration of those words demonstrated her resolve that the appropriate moment for Jesus to act had come. The acceptable time had arrived, and Jesus came to share in her understanding. The party continued with the best wine served at the end.

In this passage we hear the mother of the adult Jesus speak, and we hear her as a powerful person with a clear, prophetic awareness of the fullness of time. Even when Jesus questions her purpose and timing, it is clear that she perceives this time and occasion as the appropriate ones for him to demonstrate who he is. Indeed, timing is an important aspect throughout the story. It begins, "On the third day there was a wedding in Cana of Galilee." This clear chronological note is in marked contrast to Mary's perception. It is not *chronos,* or the passage of time, with its measurable duration that she notes. She is alert to *kairos,* a Greek word meaning "the favorable or decisive point," the awareness of time when the eternity of God has entered our minutes, hours, and days.

The third day is also significant in two other events from scripture. One is when God hands down the law at Sinai "on the third day," and the other, even more significant event is the Resurrection. Alongside Mary's perception of *kairos,* she is also clearly eager to make the wedding an occasion of untroubled celebration. She wants to shield the joyous from worry and embarrassment. She prompts Jesus to his first miracle, and he listens to her, even as the servants listen to him. There is assurance in her manner and voice, and we can follow a clear line between the young woman who received and acted on God's announcement, the prophet of the Magnificat, and the seasoned prophet who was a wedding guest at Cana. In each of those instances, Mary accepted and celebrated the presence of the saving God among us, and each event hailed the new relationship that was being forged between God and God's people. Mary as prophet stands at the door of these wondrous beginnings, and as we turn now to explore her as matriarch, we will see that she has begun a journey both unrepeatable and, in many ways, recognizably commonplace.

QUESTIONS FOR STUDY, PRAYER, AND REFLECTION

1. Can you recall an announcement or annunciation in your life? Who were the messengers and what did they tell you? How did you respond? Could God be calling you now to some new endeavor?

2. If you needed support during a time of spiritual trial, to whom

would you turn? Can you recall when someone turned to you for spiritual support?

3. Jesus said a prophet's voice is not often recognized in his own country. Voices of minorities, the poor, and women are less frequently heard and valued. What prophetic voices have you heard, what were the issues, and how did you respond to them? If God had called you to be a part of God's plan, would you align yourself with the poor and oppressed?

4. In a sense, each new commitment to Christ can be likened to a virgin birth; it is a creation brought about by God and the human soul. Christ also can bring freshness to tired and damaged relationships, to the back rooms, backyards, and stables of our lives. Where might you pray for a virgin birth in your life? What might you do to bring it to life?

5. Great events such as births and weddings are among the most joyous we experience. We see two examples of Mary seizing and celebrating joy—in singing the Magnificat and in urging Jesus to change the water into wine. How do you seize and celebrate joy in your life? Do you recall a time in your life when water was changed into wine? Who or what brought it about?

3 🦢 As Matriarch

And she gave birth to her firstborn son and wrapped him
in bands of cloth, and laid him in a manger, because there
was no place for them in the inn. (Luke 2:7)

MOSES AND HIS MOTHER AT THE NILE

She has pitched the woven papyrus
with thickened bitumen so the crossings won't leak.
She lowers the hull among the blue iris
striped petals brush his round, sleeping cheek.

Nursing is necessary to keep him quiet;
she prays he won't cry since no muffling would mask it.
She wrests round the carrying sling to untie it
then settles him deeply into the basket.

Tucking beneath him the warm, patterned weaving,
she dries sticky sweetness that drips from her breast,
then signals her young sentry daughter she's leaving,
and wades, with skirts floating, the river's wide crest.

She tightens the bindings cushioned with wool
as reeds underwater undulate, pull.

MISSING THE MOTHER

I remember going to visit my aunt in Ohio several years ago. She asked about my daughter at home, then in elementary school. I said my daughter was fine but was missing her mother. My aunt responded, "I think we always miss our mother." Such longing is, I think, also true of the church. Though we know intellectually that God transcends gender and could be called both Mother and Father, Jesus' use of the intimate word for father, *Abba,* still prevails, and that leaves for many the longing for a heavenly mother. Consequently many Christians have turned to Mary, the flesh-and-blood mother in our story of faith. One woman described her upbringing as "Maryless," and her coined word speaks volumes about the need Mary has filled over the centuries. Though Mary is not the only image of motherhood in the Judeo-Christian story, she conveys a powerful image of devoted maternal care. We all want to have someone who delights in our being and has our best interests in mind, someone who is connected to us, heart, body, and soul. Such a person often is one's mother. A story from my own family lore tells of such a mother:

My grandfather's cousin and his wife, Mary, had one son, Charles, who at twelve had gone fifty miles away from home to a Boy Scout camp. Back in the 1920s in southern Ohio, fifty miles was a pretty long distance, and few people had telephones, let alone today's instant and constant communication. Charles was in good health and had been gone only a few days when one morning at 3:00 A.M., his mother wakened and told her husband to get up, there was something wrong with Charles. Her husband said she had just had a bad dream and urged her to go back to sleep, but she persisted. She said she knew her son needed her and she had to go. Finally, she said that if he would not drive her—and she didn't drive—she would find someone else who would. So her husband got up, thinking it was crazy, and drove her to the camp. When they arrived the scoutmaster was astonished. He said the boy was very sick, and he was greatly relieved to see them, but he was bewildered as to how they had known to come. Charles had spinal meningitis, and died hours later. When her child had needed her, Mary had known it and found the means to get to him.

OTHER MOTHERS IN THE HEBREW BIBLE

Although some may see the biblical Mary as solitary and unique, she was part of a community, and her first action after the Annunciation was to seek out the help and companionship of another woman. She had been raised on stories of mothers, and no doubt was influenced by those other women whose lives were woven into scripture. Who might those women be?

First, of course, would be Eve, so named by Adam because she was "the mother of all living." Mary has often been called "the new Eve," the one who overturned the curse brought about by the first parents' disobedience. Yet Phyllis Trible, a biblical scholar, has pointed out that although Eve usually has been cast as the one who succumbed to temptation, recent scholarship shows that both she and Adam share that responsibility. A phrase in Genesis that had been omitted by Jerome in the fourth century, and left out until the New Revised Standard Version of 1989, says, "And she also gave some to her husband, *who was with her*, and he ate."[1] Eve was clearly a responsible party in that first disobedience, and one attracted to knowledge, power, and the taste of beautiful fruit. But the long-neglected phrase "who was with her" shows Adam's complicity and finally sets the record straight.

In addition to eating from the tree of the knowledge of good and evil, Eve was a mother, and more particularly, the mother of Cain and Abel. She experienced the death of her second son at the hands of her first son, and the subsequent exile of the son that remained. She had already lost paradise once, and more was torn from her with violence and sibling enmity. While scripture does not mention her grief, the death of her child was the first mother's loss, and became a kinship Mary would later share with her.

Throughout history Mary has been shown in contrast to Eve. As the first created woman (and, significantly, the final creature that God created), Eve was responsible with Adam for the fall of humanity. She represented the old creation, and as such she stood in contrast to Mary, who was shown as ushering in a new, redeemed creation. Just as Eve stood beneath the tree of the knowledge of good and evil taking the forbidden fruit, so Mary stood beneath the cross, having given the fruit of her body for the salvation of the ruined world. Mary has been seen as the mother of a new creation—the church—because she was the mother of Christ and the church is the Body of Christ.

But long before theologians began to compare the two women, long before Eve was demonized and Mary was exalted, Mary was a Hebrew girl hearing the stories of scripture and feeling in her own mornings something of the freshness of the garden of Eden. She was learning from the teachings in the second chapter of Genesis both the wonder of being created and the danger of pride. Perhaps the best view of Eve is the one that imagination takes, and it is wonderfully exemplified in Michelangelo's fresco in the Sistine Chapel of the creation of Adam. While most of us are familiar with the famous hands of Adam and God about to touch, fewer have noticed that among the clouds, God embraces with his other arm a young woman, who looks out at her future mate with amazed and unabashed interest.

Another mother whose story was part of Mary's world was Sarah, the first of the matriarchs and the spouse of Abraham, who is mentioned in the Magnificat and to whom God promised again and again that he would be the father of a great nation. Abraham's story, found in Genesis, chapters 11–25, tells of his marriage to Sarah, who, despite God's promise, continued to be barren. It was not a smooth marriage, and Abraham was often more concerned with his own welfare than that of his wife (twice passing her off as his sister to lie in other men's beds so he would be unharmed). We learn that Sarah was beautiful and felt the sting of her childlessness. When her maidservant, Hagar, at Sarah's suggestion, conceived a child by Abraham, Sarah was jealous and treated her harshly, adding cruelty to exploitation.

When Abraham was ninety-nine, he had an annunciation. God came to him by the oaks at Mamre and told him that in the spring Sarah, now well past menopause, would have a son. Sarah laughed, but God asked, "Is anything too wonderful for the LORD?"[2] which echoed the angel's words to Mary, "For nothing will be impossible with God."[3] The child of promise did come, and they named him Isaac, which means "laughter," because Sarah had laughed. From the story of Sarah's laughter, Mary knew that God could at times surprise us with unexpected gifts, and even be uproariously funny. To imagine Mary laughing like her foremother is to give her some of the earthiness that as mother of the one who embodied the fullness of life, she surely had and her memory deserves.

Mary knew the story of Abraham and Sarah, and she also knew the story of the test God gave to Abraham, asking him to sacrifice his son and then at the last minute replacing the child with a sacrificial ram. How she would have understood that story at the end of her life, we will never know, nor will we ever know Sarah's reaction. Scripture does not record Sarah's response to Abraham's test, but we may be confident that if she knew of it, it tested her at least as thoroughly as it did her husband.

Other stories of motherhood fill the Hebrew Bible: Rebecca's wily preference for Jacob, Rachel's two late-born sons (the last of which cost her her life), but one unnamed mother may have found particular resonance with Mary. That woman is the mother of Moses, Aaron, and Miriam. Part of her story is echoed in the poem that opens this chapter. Hers is a particularly intriguing story that nourished the occupied people of first-century Israel:

When the Israelites were in Egypt, they had grown so strong as a people that the Egyptian pharaoh was concerned, and he gave them hard, relentless labor to weaken them. This did not debilitate them, so Pharaoh took more radical measures and told the Hebrew midwives to kill the male children the moment they were born. But the midwives were clever and fooled Pharaoh, and managed to let the children live. Then, as a further resort, Pharaoh decided that all male children were to be thrown into the Nile and drowned. But the mother of Moses did not drown her son; rather, she put her child into a woven basket and set him among the reeds. Her daughter kept watch to see what would happen. Pharaoh's daughter found the child and took pity on him. Then the daughter who kept watch—very likely Miriam, who was Mary's namesake—asked Pharaoh's daughter if she could go and find a nurse for the child among the Hebrew people. The princess agreed, and the shrewd girl brought her own mother to nurse the child.

The story of Moses was a vitally important one to the people of Israel. He was their liberator, and during the time of Mary, the Jews were once more living under another nation's rule. Mary must have known the story of the infant Moses among the bulrushes, and must have seen in his mother's action both the trust that would release that baby into the threatening world and the clever planning that would make that world as safe as possible.

What other mothers had been woven into Mary's understanding of motherhood? We know of one for certain: Hannah, the mother of Samuel the prophet, because she spoke words that Mary would later echo in the Magnificat. Her story, found in First Samuel, chapters 1–2, tells of an infertile woman who longs for a child. She prayed so fervently for a son (and promised that if she had a son she would give him to God) that Eli, the temple priest, assumed she was drunk. When he chastised her, she explained the source of her anxiety, and Eli asked God to hear her plea. Hannah conceived, and true to a promise she had made, after the child Samuel was weaned, she presented him to the temple. When she gave Samuel to Eli, she prayed, speaking words that celebrated God's preference for the hungry, the poor, and the needy, and the reversal that would come for the rich and powerful. Mary would have known Hannah's story, her sacrificing motherhood, and most clearly, her prayer or song:

My heart exults in the LORD;
my strength is exalted in my God.
My mouth derides my enemies,
because I rejoice in my victory.

. . . The bows of the mighty are broken,
but the feeble gird on strength.
Those who were full have hired themselves out for bread,
but those who were hungry are fat with spoil.

The barren has borne seven,
but she who has many children is forlorn. . . .
The LORD makes poor and makes rich;
he brings low, he also exalts.
He raises up the poor from the dust;
he lifts the needy from the ash heap,
to make them sit with princes
and inherit a seat of honor.[4]

Hannah's prayer not only inspired Mary and was echoed in her Magnificat; it also marked a significant change in temple life. The main reason Eli thought Hannah was drunk was because prior to her prayer, there had been no private prayer in the temple; it had been a place for communal prayer and public oration. It also had been a communal gathering place for ritual and animal sacrifice. Hannah's personal prayer marked the transformation of the House of God to a House of Prayer,[5] a distinction that Jesus would later fight to preserve.

It is important to remember that when Mary gave birth to Jesus, she gave him not only her flesh and blood but also a family and social context. Mary was a Jewish woman, and like her own mother did for her, she instructed Jesus in the culture of his people. She was his first teacher, and the stories of the mothers of her faith were part of their legacy. As she repeated the stories to her child, she probably heard them with new ears befitting her new situation and charge.

THE BIRTH OF JESUS

Mary's own story, the story of the birth of Jesus, occurs in only two of the four gospels. The earliest gospel, the Gospel of Mark, begins with Jesus' baptism by John the Baptist, and the Gospel of John presents Jesus as preexistent, from the beginning of time. It is only Matthew and Luke, with their very different perspectives on the Nativity, that tell us anything about Jesus' beginnings. Scholars believe that those two gospels were written backward, that is, the birth narratives were set down after the stories of the death and Resurrection of Jesus. Luke claims that his account was handed on to him from those who were eyewitnesses, and because his account details the experiences of Mary, some traditions have viewed the early chapters of Luke as memoirs of Mary, but that view has not survived the scrutiny of biblical scholarship.[6] The birth narratives also may have come in response to the Docetic heresy, which proclaimed, among other things, that Jesus arrived on earth fully mature.

The gospels are not historical documents, though historical material is found in them. Neither are they innocuous stories; rather, they tell pointedly and at counterpoint of Herod's massacre and the gentile Magi, of the Pax Romana and the Prince of Peace, of the named rulers (Augustus and Quirinius) and the unnamed shepherds.[7] They are essentially proclamations of faith, with a truth found in myth and folktale that educates the soul and tells us who we are. Regardless of the ways in which, or the reasons for which, they were written, the stories of the birth of Jesus bring their own depths of wisdom and spirituality that continue to nourish believers in every generation.

Matthew's gospel places the birth within the context of the Hebrew prophets. He says, "The birth of Jesus the Messiah took place in this way . . . to fulfill what had been spoken by the Lord through the prophet: "Look, the virgin shall conceive and bear a son, and they shall name him 'Emmanuel,' which means 'God is with us.'"[8] Matthew is referring to the prophet Isaiah and the passage that reads: "Therefore the Lord himself will give you a sign. Look, the young woman is with child and shall bear a son, and shall name him Immanuel."[9] Matthew uses the word *virgin* because he was quoting from a Greek translation of Isaiah, while the Hebrew original (from which the New Revised Standard Version is translated) uses the term *young woman*. The variation between the two has given rise to some of the most heated debates in the history of biblical scholarship.

Essentially, much of the debate has focused on an understanding of prophecy: whether prophecy meant a prediction of future events or a challenge to live more in accordance with God's will. Contemporary scholarship and theology support the latter view. It is now generally understood that the prophet Isaiah was not describing the manner in which the promised child would be conceived, but rather that the child would come when Israel's fortunes had reached their lowest ebb. Isaiah understood that God acts in history, because that had been clearly shown in the exodus from Egypt, but Isaiah had not foreseen the conception by the Holy Spirit, and, as such, his writing did not predict the virgin birth.[10]

Matthew tells of the pregnancy and birth from Joseph's perspective:

> When his mother Mary had been engaged to Joseph, but before they lived together, she was found to be with child from the Holy Spirit. Her husband Joseph, being a righteous man and unwilling to expose her to public disgrace, planned to dismiss her quietly. But just when he had resolved to do this, an angel of the Lord appeared to him in a dream and said, "Joseph, son of David, do not be afraid to take Mary as your wife, for the child conceived in her is from the Holy Spirit. She will bear a son, and you are to name him Jesus, for he will save his people from their sins." All this took place to fulfill what had been spoken by the Lord through the prophet:
> "Look, the virgin shall conceive
> and bear a son,
> and they shall name him
> Emmanuel,"
> which means "God is with us." When Joseph awoke from sleep, he did as the angel of the Lord commanded him; he took her as his wife, but had no marital relations with her until she had borne a son; and he named him Jesus.[11]

This passage points out the vulnerability of Mary's situation and gives us a glimpse into the character and spirituality of Joseph. It is important to realize that betrothal in Jewish society meant that the couple was promised to each other, but normally there was a waiting period of one year before the wedding, during which the couple would begin to live together in marriage. Mary's pregnancy could have easily been construed as adultery because she was pledged to Joseph, and the official punishment for adultery was death by stoning. Even if such punishment was not always carried out, this clearly was a crisis situation. The passage also suggests that their marital arrangement was a normal sexual one, for Matthew says that they had no marital relations until after the birth, which implies that they did have marital relations afterward.

WOMEN IN FIRST-CENTURY JEWISH SOCIETY

It is important to see Mary within the context of women during her period of history. The situation was one of male power and dominance in the family, in society, and in the temple. A young woman was under the power of her father until that power was transferred to her husband. At marriage she became her husband's property, and he paid a sum of money, or dowry, for her. A father even had the right to sell his daughter as a slave up until the age of twelve. Up to that age, she had no right to refuse a husband that her father had chosen for her, and a father often chose the husband, because a dowry was a significant source of income.

Once married, a woman's worth was determined by her capacity for childbearing, and male children were valued more highly than female children. Because her standing in society was dependent on the men in her life, her education was limited. In addition, she had no rights to succession or inheritance, as did male children, and this further maintained her dependency. Should a woman seek to end her marriage, divorce laws favored the man, which further diminished her power. If she was widowed, levirate marriage laws meant that a widow was bound to marry a brother of her dead husband; otherwise she could not remarry. While this offered some protection for a widow, it also limited her choices. Other laws, both secular and religious, curtailed a woman's freedom. For example, she could not bear witness, was forbidden to teach, and was kept far from the altar during worship. Politically, economically, and in many of the social spheres, women were prohibited from taking an active part. An indication of the lowly status of women is in the traditional morning prayer in which male Jews thank God for not making them infidels, uneducated, slaves, or women.[12]

Jesus ushered in a new understanding of the value of women. He spoke to them, respected them, and raised them above the status the culture gave them. As a result, and not surprisingly, his followers included many women. Jesus' treatment of women also tells us something about his mother. As his first teacher, she may well have challenged the prevailing view of women. Perhaps as a consequence of that, Jesus treated women as intelligent and capable people, regardless of their status. He spoke easily with them (as with the woman at the well),[13] praising them for cleverness (as he did the Syrophoenician woman),[14] for faith (as he did the woman with the hemorrhage),[15] and for hospitality (as he did the woman who anointed him).[16]

MOTHERHOOD

It is helpful for our understanding to put Mary into the context of all new mothers, and Joseph into the context of all new fathers. Pregnancy is both a glorious and a disturbing time in a woman's life, and for her husband as well. Her body changes, having a new life of its own. Her sleep is disrupted, her appetite is changed; she can be either nauseous or ravenous. Her husband is concerned for her and for his growing responsibilities, wondering what kind of father he will be and if he can support his growing family. She has trouble balancing the weight she is carrying. And she worries. Childbirth stories abound among women. She knows the delivery will be painful, but doesn't know the extent. She knows many women and infants die in childbirth, and wonders if she and her baby will survive. All Mary knew from the angel messenger was that she would bear a son. The rest was mystery, though mystery with some human predictability. There was a good likelihood that the night of the birth would not be a silent night: there are usually at least two vocal participants!

For Mary, as for all mothers, much more is in store after the child is born. Children quite simply change a person's life as almost nothing else can. An infant is a full-time job. Someone must spend their time feeding, changing, cleaning, and comforting the baby. Matthew's gospel tells us that Mary and Joseph had little time to adjust to the newborn before they had unexpected guests. The Magi, those wise ones who were probably Zoroastrians from Persia and had followed the star, seeking the new king, arrived soon after the birth. And shepherds from the nearby fields came as well. The Magi brought gifts of gold, frankincense, and myrrh, gifts rich in symbolism and befitting a king. We know little about the Magi, yet they traditionally are shown representing several races, to indicate the Gentile world. And at least one stained-glass window has broadened the representation to show one of the gift-bearing visitors as a woman.[17]

Mary and Joseph would have received the gifts on behalf of the child. They were strange and symbolic gifts—most unlike the practical gifts of today's baby showers. Gold represents the currency of this world and kingship; frankincense speaks of purification and worship; and myrrh is a burial spice. Mary received the gifts, and she may have influenced the way in which Jesus came to understand them. Jesus did not interpret events or understand things as the Jews or first Gentile followers expected. He did not seek wealth or kingship but taught radical sharing; he did not yield to the pressure to become an object of worship but rather gave an example of servanthood. He did not succumb to death but wrenched himself free of the grave.[18] It is clear that the gifts, which were meant as tribute, were significant in the way Jesus viewed his purpose. But the Magi were not the only visitors, and the shepherds from the fields, who also came to the stable, may have influenced Jesus' sense of himself as well. In time he would come to differentiate between the good shepherd and the hireling, and eventually would understand himself as the good shepherd who would lay down his life for his sheep.

It is interesting to note that, millions of Christmas cards to the contrary, no oxen and sheep are mentioned in the gospel accounts of the Nativity, and not even the very probable donkey is actually in scripture. Tradition alone insists that they were there, perhaps as a reminder that human birth is not unlike birth for other mammals. The presence of the manger mentioned in scripture would indicate domestic animals. The gospel does say that Mary laid Jesus in a manger, a story she probably recounted to him over and over, as family lore evolves in all families. No doubt it fastened in his mind and factored in his understanding of himself. Having once lain in a manger where beasts are fed may have stirred his awareness of the common human bond of sustenance, and influenced his own genius in conceiving the Eucharist. Despite the limited biblical description of the Nativity, the prevailing image of the birth is one of a young family surrounded by animals. And no matter how often some artists would render the Madonna and child as ethereal, others insist on the donkey, the ox, and the lamb.

But regardless of the many ways in which Mary was depicted, she was hurled, like all new mothers, into the hectic, disruptive, clamorous, and wonderful world of young children. According to the Gospel of Matthew, during her early motherhood, she had the additional burden of fleeing the hostile political forces of King Herod. She had to learn to be a mother while in flight as a refugee. Hers was motherhood on the move, and as refugees must often travel in secret, hiding an infant whose primary means of communicating is his cry was a huge and often repeated challenge.

RELIGIOUS RITUALS FOLLOWING THE BIRTH

The Gospel of Luke gives us a more placid view of the Holy Family's early life, and tells us of the events that followed the birth: the circumcision of Jesus and his presentation in the temple at Jerusalem. The trip to the temple to present Jesus had a dual purpose, because Mary also went for the customary purification that was required of women after childbirth.[19] A woman who bore a male child was considered ritually unclean for seven days following the birth, and she would have been expected to remain in ceremonial isolation for an additional thirty-three days, for a total of forty days (or eighty days for a female child), and she was forbidden to touch anything consecrated or to enter the sanctuary. At the temple a woman was required to present to the priest a lamb for a burnt offering and a dove for a sin offering, or two doves if she was poor. Mary and Joseph, being poor, offered the latter.

> When the time came for their purification according to the law of Moses, they brought him up to Jerusalem to present him to the Lord (as it is written in the law of the Lord, "Every firstborn male shall be designated as holy to the Lord"), and they offered a sacrifice according to what is stated in the law of the Lord, "a pair of turtledoves or two young pigeons."[20]

The Feast of the Presentation is sometimes known as Candlemas, and in the Orthodox churches, it has been called the Meeting of Christ with Simeon. The focus of this ancient celebration was shifted by the late medieval church from the Presentation of Our Lord to the Purification of Mary. Actually, two separate things are taking place in this one event, and two separate rites in Judaism were conflated in the second chapter of Luke's gospel.

Clearly, medieval minds were intrigued by the purification of the virgin mother. For Mary it marked the fulfillment of the law and the end of her period of ritual isolation. She was now free to move about socially and to enter the temple. Although the period of isolation may have been helpful for rest and bonding with the child, the purification at the temple was probably an event she was pleased to see arrive.

In the 1979 revision of the Episcopal *Book of Common Prayer,* the church returned to the ancient focus of the day, the Presentation of Our Lord. Jewish law, as written in Exodus 13:2, stated that every firstborn son was to be dedicated to God in memory of the deliverance from Egypt, when the firstborn of Egypt were killed and those of ancient Israel were spared. In addition, all firstborn human beings and animals and all first fruits of the harvest were considered to belong to God. Even when the Jews were unsure of what would follow, they offered the first they had to God. The presentation of Jesus signals the meeting of the Old and New Dispensations, and despite the family offering doves for purification, it marks the end of the old system of sacrificial offerings. When Jesus was presented to Simeon, he was the perfect offering, replacing all the lambs and doves of the past.

Following the prescribed rituals, the Holy Family settled into daily life as a threesome. Family life for all human beings has consistent requirements across cultures and centuries. There would be an income to earn and a household to run. They were a poor family, and so Mary would have done the shopping, cooking, cleaning, and child care, with its constant stream of laundry and feeding. Quite possibly, she also helped with the family business. As we have seen, Mary and Joseph were observant Jews, and so her work would have circled the Sabbath and included provisions for the special feasts and fasts of the Jewish year. The following poem imagines a quiet moment in Mary's early days as a parent:

THEOTOKOS
She would sit at times and watch the white curls
of wood fall from the chisel and form a small heap beside
the mallet and she would look at the face intent
with its lines and crests and furrows.

Then she would look at the child, perfect in his
newness, and see time already chipping the shape
of his days. She would hold her knees and rock
into the blessing of those mornings already falling

from her fingers. It was the child's first summer
and, as with many mothers, heaven here on earth.

THE CHILDHOOD OF JESUS

Mary and Joseph returned to Nazareth, and the four canonical
gospels tell nothing about their next decade. But the infancy narrative of Thomas, another ancient manuscript, tells of the boyhood
of Jesus. It has strong Gnostic influences, and shows the child as a
wonder-working child, very unlike other children, but it does contain one particularly interesting story of Jesus with his mother:

> When he was six years old, his mother sent him to draw water
> and bring it back to the house. But he lost his grip on the pitcher
> in the jostling of the crowd, and it fell and broke. So Jesus spread
> out the cloak he was wearing and filled it with water and carried
> it back to his mother. His mother, once she saw the miracle that
> had occurred, kissed him; but she kept to herself the mysteries
> that she had seen him do.[21]

It is worth noting that despite the abundance of tender images of Mary and Jesus in religious art, this childhood miracle gives
the only recorded mention of physical affection between them. But
Jesus apparently had a happy childhood. As an adult he welcomed
children and encouraged his followers to become childlike, saying
they would not enter the reign of God unless they became as children.[22] He also said that those who maintained childlike innocence
and joy had access to divine wisdom.[23] From such sayings we may
assume that Jesus was loved and valued as a child, and that his
childhood was a cherished and protected time.

Many of those undocumented years would have been taken
up with family matters. We can see from the gospels that Jesus was
perceptive about the household and observed how his mother did
things. He noted how leaven made bread rise; how old fabric was
used to repair worn garments; the cost of items at the market (such
as sparrows); how moths and rust worked to frustrate even the

most meticulous homemaker; how merchants varied their mea-
sure of a bushel; and how day laborers stood waiting for work. He
learned childhood games and the prescribed roles for boys and girls:
how boys would pipe and dance as if for a wedding and girls would
wail as if for a funeral.[24] He also learned to read, because he read
from the scroll of Isaiah in the temple,[25] and one gospel story indicates he could also write.[26]

He learned how babies were born and how a woman forgot
her pain in the joy of new life. He learned something of the way
houses were made—what materials gave structural strength—and
he came to know the animals and plants of the surrounding countryside. He watched the chickens, doves, dogs, foxes, sheep, and
camels, and he noticed the wheat, tares, olive trees, fig trees,
grapevines, wild mustard, and lilies of the field. All of those obser-
vations were worked into his parables, which addressed his hear-
ers with images and stories of the world they knew.

FAMILY LIFE

Mark's gospel describes the family of Jesus from the point of view
of other townfolk. They describe Jesus as "the carpenter, the son of
Mary and brother of James and Joses and Judas and Simon," and
they also mention "his sisters."[27] Those passages give us important
information. They tell us that Mary and her family were well
known in the community, that she was a recognized member of the
town, and that plainly there were more children in her family. Jesus
had brothers and sisters, and we are given the brothers' names:
James, Joses, Judas, and Simon. While the sisters' names are not
specifically given, we are told that he had more than one.

This information has been perplexing to those Christians who
are persuaded that Mary had only one child and remained perpet-
ually a virgin. In their understanding, Joseph was a kindly protector and patron of his wife, who had consecrated her virginity to
God. Adherents of this view have explained the other children as
cousins, or children from a previous marriage of Joseph's. However,
if we accept the idea that the brothers and sisters of Jesus were in
fact children of Joseph's previous marriage, and if we recall that
Jesus' active ministry began when he was about thirty years old,

then we have the perplexing situation of four middle-aged stepsons and some stepdaughters (all of whom would have to be older than thirty) in constant company with their mother, following her from place to place in a way that would be acceptable with younger children but unusual with older children, particularly in a culture that expected people to marry early and reproduce. This becomes even more unlikely if we consider the children to be nephews and nieces.

On the other hand, if we are open to the possibility that Mary had other children (the Bible mentions at least six other children, seven including Jesus), we begin to see her as a matriarch with an active family life. In such a scenario, we would need to view Joseph and their marital arrangement differently, seeing Mary as a sexually active partner in a vital domestic scene. Though this may trouble some Christians, it is important to remember that in first-century Judaism, virginity was not consecrated (as it was in pagan religions), nor was celibacy considered a virtue. As the chosen mother of the Christ, it makes sense that she exemplified fullness of life, which, for a Jewish woman of her time, included a husband and more children. Sexuality within marriage was never viewed as a moral failure, much less a sin, and children were counted as blessings and signs of God's favor toward the mother. Virginity quite simply meant sterility. In fact, marital love is celebrated in the Song of Solomon and viewed as having potential for holiness. A contemporary couple, mindful of our current exploding population and its impact on the environment, might limit the number of their children, but such was not the concern in the first century. If we look at Mary as the center of a dynamic, bustling household, her appearances in the gospels become more easily understood. She is a busy, active part of the community, often with her children in tow. She is not only the mother of a son, but the mother of several sons and at least two daughters, whose descendants are likely among the people of Palestine today.

MARY'S SEXUALITY

Yet such ideas have been considered anathema by many. Saint Jerome, writing in the fourth century, said that the idea of other children through sex was "an outrage to the virgin."[28] Epiphanius, the fifth-century Bishop of Salamis, ardently opposed a sect in Arabia called the Antidicomarianites, or the Opponents to Mary, which held that Mary had sexual intercourse with Joseph after the birth of Jesus.[29] A more contemporary view was expressed by an Anglo-Catholic colleague who adheres to the perpetual virginity of Mary. He considered that an active sexual relationship with Joseph would nullify Mary's relationship with God or reduce it to a "one-night stand." Despite the mystery of the Annunciation, it is important to remember that a sexual encounter between God and Mary was not part of it. Although Greek and Roman myths have stories of gods and goddesses having sexual encounters with mortals, our Judeo-Christian scripture does not. The doctrine of the virgin birth holds that the conception of Jesus was an extraordinary event of parthenogenesis, which did not rule out future natural conceptions and subsequent births.

Those who have read the cited scriptural accounts of Mary may wonder about the tradition concerning Mary's lifelong virginity, because it clearly did not spring from the Bible. It is apparent from Paul's letters that he knew nothing of the miraculous birth. Though he is aware of God's intervention in a birth, such as that of Sarah, he applies the concept of a marvelous birth to Christians only in a symbolic sense, as heirs of God's promise.[30] And so what is the source of such ideas regarding Mary? The mystery is solved by one extracanonical book known as the Proevangelium, or infancy narrative, of James. Originally claimed to have been written by James the brother of Jesus (that authorship has since been disproved), the second-century book sets out in twenty-four chapters to tell the life of Mary, from her parents' conception of her until the massacre of the innocents by Herod. This document of early Christianity shows little knowledge of the traditions of women in Judaism or of Jewish temple practice, but perseveres in its task to prove the unassailable purity of the mother of Jesus.

This book describes Mary's parents, Anne and Joachim, as good and faithful people who were unable to have a child. Mary's conception came through a divine message, and when the child was born, she immediately showed wondrous qualities. Like the child Samuel in the Hebrew Bible, Mary was consecrated to the temple at an early age:

Many months passed but as the child reached two years of age, Joachim said, "Let's take her up to the temple of the Lord, so that we can keep the promise we made, or else the Lord will be angry with us and our gift will be unacceptable." And Anna said, "Let's wait until she is three, so she won't miss her father or her mother."[31]

Mary was taken to the temple, where she was warmly received, and like David she danced:

The priest welcomed her, kissed her, and blessed her: "The Lord God has exalted your name among all generations. In you the Lord will disclose his redemption to the people of Israel during the last days." And he sat her down on the third step of the altar, and the Lord showered favor on her. And she danced, and the whole house of Israel loved her.[32]

According to the Proevangelium, she was one of seven temple virgins kept by the high priest Zechariah. In the temple she led a theologically active life, almost the life of a proto-nun. Her work was weaving purple and scarlet cloth, and it was while she was in the midst of weaving that the annunciating angel appeared to her.[33] Although she had autonomy, she was under male protection. She was fed heavenly food, but as she reached puberty, there was fear she would pollute the temple (as Jewish law considered a woman ritually unclean during menstruation), and so the elderly Joseph was chosen to protect and safeguard her consecrated virginity, and she was given to him in marriage. An Orthodox variant of the story holds that Joseph accepted betrothal to Mary but hoped she would eventually give up her vow to virginity and marry one of his sons.[34]

The Proevangelium says that Mary was sixteen when the angel appeared to her. After the Annunciation and before Mary's pregnancy became apparent, a priest of the temple accused Joseph of defiling her. The couple was forced to drink a truth-telling potion, which would kill them if they were lying, and they were exonerated. The narrative continues, and tells that the birth in Bethlehem took place in a cave and that Joseph found a midwife to help. When the midwife saw that Mary remained physically a virgin after she delivered the child (with an intact hymen), the midwife proclaimed the miracle. Another woman, Salome, questioned this, and on examining Mary, her hand withered because she had doubted. Later the hand was restored when she touched the Christ child.

This extracanonical book heavily influenced the Christian understanding of Mary (interestingly, its themes are also evident in the Qur'an), and the stories it tells decorate the walls and ceilings of many ancient churches. One particularly beautiful example is the late thirteenth-, early fourteenth-century Church of Saint Savior, in Chora, outside Istanbul, Turkey, where mosaic cycles in the narthex recount Mary's life. They depict Joachim and Anne meeting, the birth of Mary, her seven first steps, her consecration, her presentation to the temple, her being fed while at the temple, and her receiving scarlet wool to weave. There is even one of her parents caressing her in a loving family group. The mosaics also illustrate her betrothal, the Nativity, and scenes from canonical gospels. One mosaic shows her dormition, or "falling asleep," which refers to her death. Though much of the Proevangelium of James has come to be understood as embroidered legend, it has nevertheless contributed material on Mary to Christianity, which for some of the faithful culminated in doctrine. It is in marked contrast to the gospels, which tell us almost nothing about Mary's birth family. Only the Gospel of John mentions that she had a sister,[35] but there is no mention of a sibling in the Proevangelium of James.

The Roman Catholic dogma of the Immaculate Conception, which claims Mary was conceived without sin, can be traced to this narrative. This dogma was proclaimed in 1854 amid much controversy. Contemporary discussions in the Roman Catholic Church over the possibility of naming Mary as "Co-Redemptrix" along with Jesus have their roots in the Immaculate Conception. But it is interesting to note that the feast of the Immaculate Conception, commemorated on December 8, was celebrated in England prior to the Norman conquest in 1066,[36] well before it was established in the East in the twelfth century and later made official in the West in the fourteenth century. It originally celebrated the importance of Saint Anne, the mother of Mary.[37] When the Pope made the Immaculate Conception dogma, the Orthodox churches rejected it as disconnecting Mary from the rest of humanity. The mainline Protestant churches dismissed it as being a nonscriptural innovation. Anglicans did not affirm or reject the doctrine, allowing for a wide variety of devotional attitudes, but also clearly resisted making it an article of faith. However, it is interesting to note that while Marian feast days have been reduced in the Episcopal Church to the Presentation of Christ in the Temple (February 2), the Annunciation (March 25), the Visitation (May 31), and the Feast of Saint Mary the Virgin (August 15), they include the Parents of the Blessed Virgin Mary (July 26). It is also worth noting that sixteen feast days are devoted to Mary in the Roman Catholic calendar for the United States.[38]

The infancy narrative of James was not officially excluded from the New Testament until 382 c.e., when the canon of the Bible was established, but it had already strongly influenced the early church on the issue of Mary's consecrated virginity. This is clear in the fourth-century writings of Saint Gregory of Nyssa:

> What is Mary's response? Listen to the voice of the pure Virgin. The angel brings the glad tidings of childbearing, but she is concerned with virginity and holds that her integrity should come before the angelic message. She does not refuse to believe the angel; neither does she move away from her convictions. She says: I have given up any contact with man. How will this happen to me, since I do not know man?"[39]

Saint Augustine was also influenced by the narrative of James. Early in the fifth century, he wrote:

> Thus Christ, in being born of a virgin who, before knowing to whom she was to give birth, had made up her mind to remain a virgin, preferred to show his approval of holy virginity rather than to impose it on her.[40]

Augustine affirms the triple virginity of Mary, writing, "a virgin conceived, a virgin gave birth, a virgin remained afterward."[41]

Yet this understanding was not always the case. Writing in the second century, possibly before the book of James was circulated, the voice of Tertullian stands out among the early church patriarchs as objecting to the idea of the perpetual virginity of Mary: "She was a virgin who gave birth to Christ, but after his birth, she was married to one man, so that both ideals of holiness might be exemplified in the parentage of Christ."[42]

Tertullian credited marriage as a different but equal route to holiness. He ascribed to Mary both the purity of the virgin state and the faithful maturity necessary to forge a genuine and lasting relationship. His understanding follows the canonical scriptures, and he comes closest to reaching a middle ground. And Helvidius of Rome, writing at the end of the fourth century, used the texts from Matthew's first chapter, which say: "Now the birth of Jesus the Messiah took place in this way. When his mother Mary had been engaged to Joseph, but before they lived together, she was found to be with child from the Holy Spirit,"[43] and that Joseph took Mary "as his wife, but had no marital relations with her until she had borne a son; and he named him Jesus."[44] These, together with Luke's gospel reference to Jesus as Mary's "firstborn son,"[45] Helvidius views as scriptural implication that Mary had additional children.[46] It is also important to remember that Saint Paul, in his letter to the Galatians, refers to "James the Lord's brother."[47]

The term *ever virgin* was applied to Mary at the Council of Chalcedon in 451, and the doctrine implied by it has been a point of orthodoxy in both the Eastern and the Roman Catholic Churches. Some have tried to hold the Anglican Church to it because of concurrence with the first four ancient church councils, but for the most part, the reformed churches have resisted this particular point.[48] The 1979 *Book of Common Prayer* rearranged the words, and Form V of the Prayers of the People refers to Mary as "the ever-blessed Virgin Mary."[49]

The spiritual dimension of virginity, a source of abounding and restorative freshness, resonates with Anglican sensibilities. However, while regeneration in the life of faith may find help in a concrete image, to focus on the perpetual physical virginity of Mary generally is not helpful to an Anglican perspective. It has served to make Mary remote from the human condition. It has also created a picture of the Holy Family that does not validate normal marriage and actually denigrates active female sexuality. If we view a spouse as one who enables her or his partner to live in a state of re-creative abundance, one who helps the beloved recapture the childlike wonder that is the spiritual dimension of virginity, then we can view the

Holy Family as a model for marriage, and one that illustrates marriage as sacrament. But if we adhere to physical virginity in Mary and a celibate marriage in the Holy Family, we lose the Holy Family's relevance for true communion in marriage. We have singled out physical love as base and inferior to the other aspects of marriage, and in doing so, we imply that the design of our bodies and God's plan in creation are suspect and best overcome. An alternative view is to assume that the mother of Jesus joyfully inhabited her body and expressed love for which the human body was made.

Before we explore how Mary understood God acting in her life, in her marriage and family, and in the other dimensions of her life, it is worth noting that Jesus often used the image of the wedding and the bridegroom in his parables. In the parable of the wedding banquet, he used the image of a wedding as synonymous with the reign of God.[50] It is clear that he was not implying a celibate union but the traditional Jewish marriage of the first century. We can assume that his image of a marriage was based first and foremost on the marriage that he knew best, that of Mary and Joseph. It is time to restore full humanity to the Holy Family and celebrate the ways that Mary, as maiden, wife, and mother, nurtured her husband and children, and through them, the church.

QUESTIONS FOR STUDY, PRAYER, AND REFLECTION

1. What experience of your mother is the most affirming one you can recall? What experience is the most disappointing? What is your image of a good mother?
2. In your own life, did you experience a fall from grace? Was your own pride involved? What do you have in common with Eve? with Adam? with Mary?
3. How do you understand your faith in relation to marriage? sexuality? children? How are they related?
4. Because early church theologians battled the cults of pagan fertility goddesses, do you see a correlation between such concerns and the perpetual virginity of Mary?
5. Do you think the stories of Mary's early life might have had a different emphasis if they had been written by a woman? Explain. How would you illustrate the Nativity scene?

4 🕭 As Theologian

His mother treasured all these things in her heart. (Luke 2:51)

GLORY

Can you imagine them after the birth?
Poor ones, even with the ornate tribute, he
leading her with the infant on the droop-eared donkey.
Even if an aureole shone like the gold of the magus,
it would need to be enshrouded.
There would be no hosannas for this journey,
just the secret, winding way south of the city,
and the dry route to Egypt, watching their backs.

As she looked at the sky with its robe of stars
and the child swaddled in strips of rags, perhaps
she wondered about a God whose economies
would trade eternity for a length of days,
and lavish rays of heaven's glory on a hay crib
in a stable among tired, bewildered beasts.

Mary's Point of View

Human beings down the ages have struggled to understand their experiences of the divine, so we might wonder how Mary understood hers. As a prophet she had been seized by God and spoke for the divine; but she also pondered God and God's actions in her life from other perspectives. Her experiences as a wife and mother challenged her and called her to comprehend, integrate, and even systematize the way she understood God acting in her life.

Like Mary, it can be demanding for us to understand our lives in relation to God's will. What does God want of us? Are we following the right path? What is God's plan for us? We pray, study, meditate, and wait for clues and clarity. I recall my first year at seminary and a conversation in the dormitory kitchen. Different people were reflecting on their route to ministry and how God had called them. Grand moments were recounted, moments of realization, encouragement, and confirmation. After everyone had left, I sat in the kitchen with one other woman and sheepishly admitted that I had received no such clear call. My classmate may have perceived my worry as she paused, looked at me, and flatly said, "Well, you're here, aren't you?"

How did Mary understand herself and her experience of God? If *theology* is defined as "the study of the nature of God and religious truth,"[1] then Mary must have been engaged in theology, trying, like me that day in the dormitory kitchen, to make sense of what was happening in her life, what God was doing in the person of the child she had borne. Theology is actually less the formulation of doctrine and more the theory of Christian experience. Unlike the simple practice of religion, it has a reflective dimension. It may seem to be a leap to call Mary a theologian, especially if we think of a theologian as someone with an advanced degree. But we all do theology, we all find God in the events of our lives, in family, in friends, in the daily experiences of living, and in being a body, soul, mind, and heart in this created world. Like us, Mary pondered and searched for meaning and understanding. She considered, weighed, contemplated, mused, studied, meditated, examined. In doing so she did theology.

In the sixteenth century, Richard Hooker developed a three-fold base for authority in the Anglican tradition. That base was scripture, tradition, and reason. They became important components of theological understanding, and they still offer helpful ways of understanding ourselves in relation to God. The Methodist Quadrilateral added experience to that base, and experience has become an identifying mark of much contemporary theology. From a foundation that was primarily European and male, feminist theology looks at the lived experience of women as crucial material in formulating an inclusive and contemporary theology. Black and Latino theologians, as well as those from the Pacific rim, also include their unique ethnic experience to inform theology. Gay, lesbian, bisexual, and transgender voices add to the chorus claiming the importance of experience in formulating theology that speaks for all people created in the image of God. The four areas of scripture, tradition, reason, and experience functioned in people's lives in the first century as they do in ours. By exploring each one in relation to Mary's life and times, we can gain a picture of the way in which her ponderings and theological reflections were shaped.

SCRIPTURE

How might Mary have understood her life in light of the scripture she knew? How did she make sense of the Annunciation? There were biblical stories of women who longed for children, such as Sarah and Hannah, and stories of women who mothered leaders, such as the mother of Moses, but where did her story fit? Given the precarious nature of her pregnancy, perhaps she discovered understanding in the annals of women who found themselves on the boundaries of society. Scripture tells of a number of such women, but four are particularly relevant because they are listed in Matthew's genealogy of Jesus. Mary is first mentioned at the end of that long genealogy, which concludes, "and Matthan the father of Jacob, and Jacob the father of Joseph the husband of Mary, of whom Jesus was born, who is called the Messiah."[2] It is interesting that the genealogy linking Jesus with David goes through Joseph's line. The evangelists saw Davidic paternity given not through natural fatherhood but through legal fatherhood. When Joseph did not divorce Mary but assumed public responsibility for her and the child, he assumed legal paternity. Also, and more important, he named the child, following the angelic instruction in his dream, "You are to name him Jesus."[3] In doing so he acknowledged the child as his own son.

It is also important to note that the language changes when Matthew comes to Jesus. There is a strong pattern of "—, the father of —, and —, the father of —," which is broken with "Joseph the husband of Mary, of whom Jesus was born." This is because Joseph was not the biological father of Jesus. It is through Joseph that Jesus is begotten as a son of David, as it is through Mary that Jesus is begotten as a son of God.[4] Some rabbinical writing from the fourth century suggests that Mary was descended from "princes and rulers" but "played the harlot with carpenters." It is possible that the authors, despite their efforts to discredit Jesus' mother's virtue, accepted Matthew's genealogy, and seeing that Joseph was not the father, put the royal lineage on Mary's side.[5]

Matthew's genealogy follows the men down the generations from Abraham to Jesus, but the evangelist has chosen to mention and include four women along with their husbands. He might have included the names of Sarah, Rebecca, and Rachel, but he did not. Instead he included four women who had questionable but firm relationships to Israel's covenant with God: Tamar, Rahab, Ruth, and Bathsheba. Each of these stories has something irregular and even scandalous in it. Each of these four women could be viewed as a foreigner, and each forged through difficult and unusual means—almost by hook and by crook—her own central place in the history of salvation. These four of David's line quite possibly interested the young wife of that esteemed lineage and may have figured in her theology. We will look at each of the foremothers in some depth as we try to understand how Mary understood herself in light of the Messiah's lineage.

TAMAR

There are two Tamars in the Hebrew Bible: one is a Canaanite woman and the other is a daughter of King David. The ancestor of Jesus is a Canaanite woman who has married the son of Judah. Judah, you may recall, was a son of Jacob, and the one who figured prominently in selling his brother Joseph into slavery in Egypt. In fact, the story of Tamar occurs in Genesis, chapter 38, following the story of Joseph being sold by his brothers.

Judah had three sons, and Tamar married the firstborn. But scripture says the first son did evil, and God brought about his death. According to levirate law, the widow then bears progeny by the second son. Levirate marriage law might seem odd to us because the children born are attributed to the dead brother, not the living one. But the second son, whose name was Onan, resisted providing children for his dead brother and instead "spilled his semen on the ground."[6] God was displeased with him, and he was put to death also.

Judah told Tamar that she should remain a widow in his house until the youngest son was old enough to provide her with children, but Judah was afraid that his last son would die like the others, and so, even when the son came of age, he did not give the surviving son to Tamar. Meanwhile Judah's wife had died, and Tamar, perceiving the situation and determined to bear a child, veiled herself like a temple prostitute and met her father-in-law beside the road. She negotiated with him and arranged to take his staff, cord, and signet ring as a pledge for her services. It is important to note that while Tamar and Judah were not actual blood kin, such an act would be termed incestuous.

Several months later it became clear that Tamar was pregnant, and Judah called for her to be burned to death for her unchasteness. As she was brought out to be killed, she sent her father-in-law his staff, cord, and signet ring, with the word that "it was the owner of these who made me pregnant." Judah acknowledged them, and admitted, "She is more in the right than I, since I did not give her to my son."[7]

Tamar was determined to have the child that her husband's religion promised. In *The Female Ancestors of Christ,* Ann Belford Ulanov explains that God had selected Tamar, who had come from the fertility religions, because her fierce maternal determination was bound to produce a link in the unbroken line of salvation.[8] Tamar represents the primordial power of female sexuality, which can be dangerous, out-of-bounds, and impersonal, yet it is through her daring and insistence that sexuality and spirituality are woven together in the genealogical line of Jesus. Perhaps Mary found in Tamar the courage to face shame and the hope of eventual vindication. Joseph had not believed her until God spoke to him in a dream, just as Judah had not believed Tamar until she showed him his staff, cord, and signet ring. Tamar's story and her bravery in the face of humiliation may have been a sign of hope for Mary during those difficult days.

It is interesting to note in this context Jesus' treatment of a woman he considered to be outside his mission to the nation of Israel. In his encounter with the Syrophoenician, or Canaanite, woman, he not only applauded her clever use of argument, but went on to change his mind.[9] It is the only instance in the gospels where he did so, and it was in response to the challenge of a woman not unlike his bold foremothers. Could knowledge of his foreign ancestors have added to her plea? It is significant that she argued for inclusion, and that after his encounter with her, Jesus broadened his mission to include the Gentile world.

RAHAB

Rahab is the second woman ancestor that Matthew names. Her story is found in the second chapter of Joshua. While Tamar played the part of a temple prostitute to conceive a child, Rahab was the genuine article, a working whore in the city of Jericho. The story takes place after the Israelites had wandered forty years in the desert looking for the Promised Land. Joshua sent two spies to map out the Canaanite territories, and they lodged with Rahab in a house near the town wall. But the spies were reported and authorities searched the town.

Rahab hid them under flax drying on her roof, then made terms with them. She had heard the spies talking of the God of Israel, and she figured out both the relative strengths of the opposing armies and the strengths of the faiths they represented, and she chose to cast her lot with the Israelites. She was clearly a thoughtful and perceptive woman. After recounting what she had heard about the Red Sea and their other victories to the spies, she told them, "As soon as we heard it, our hearts melted, and there was no courage left in any of us because of you."[10] Her words are echoed in the Magnificat, in which Mary says, "He has scattered the proud in the thoughts of their hearts." Rahab asked that the Israelites save her as she had saved them. They told her to tie a crimson cord to her window and put all her family inside her house and she would be safe. So when Jericho was attacked and fell, only Rahab and her family survived.

Rahab was like Tamar in that she was a Canaanite woman. She was a foreigner, but even more of an outsider because she was also a prostitute, one outside the lines of respectable society. She was a wily, canny kind of person, concerned for her own skin and loyal only to her kin, but she had heard of a God who parted the Red Sea and drowned Egyptians in protecting his people, and she was drawn to that God. What she did involved huge risk. If the Canaanites had won, we can assume she would have met a horrible death as a traitor, and her whole family with her. Many people would have been paralyzed by indecision, but Rahab was able to embrace the new with a childlike faith. Despite the fact that she worked as a prostitute, there was an independence and even a purity about her. She did not define herself in terms of her relationships, but rather in the truth she recognized. Tenacity and shrewdness like Rahab's may have been necessary for Mary when she needed to protect her child from the maneuvers and mayhem of Herod.

The poem that opens this chapter imagines Mary's thoughts as the Holy Family flees to Egypt. Though we don't usually think of Mary as outwitting adversaries, she clearly needed to do so at times. A medieval legend attributes strategy and cleverness to her: It tells of her stopping to speak with a farmer on the flight into Egypt. He was sowing and planting, and Mary was aware that soldiers were close behind them. She asked the farmer to tell the soldiers that he had seen the Holy Family as he was planting. He agreed, and she went on. Moments later his field had sprouted and was growing rapidly. Just moments after that, it was ready for harvest. He was harvesting when the soldiers came by, and, as promised, he told them that he had seen the Holy Family when he was planting. The stunned soldiers turned back. Though this story may have its origins in legends of a pagan grain goddess, it also offers us a fresh perspective on Mary as a wily protector of her child.[11]

In Hebrews, chapter 11, Rahab is extolled as an example of obedience with these words: "By faith Rahab the prostitute did not perish with those who were disobedient,"[12] and she went on to marry into the line of Abraham and become an ancestor to the redeemer of the world. Jesus may have been aware of his foremother Rahab as an example of faith. He noted the faith of outcasts, and remarked that it was tax collectors and prostitutes who first believed and would precede others in entering God's realm.[13]

RUTH

Ruth is the best known of the women ancestors, and the Book of Ruth is one of the great stories of friendship in the Bible. Some scholars believe that the book was authored by a woman because it so clearly represents the female point of view and voices the underside of patriarchy.[14] The story takes place when the Judges ruled and there was a famine. A man of Bethlehem in Judah, Elimelech, took his wife, Naomi, and two sons and went to live in Moab. Elimelech died and the two sons married Moabite women, Orpah and Ruth, and then, within ten years, both sons died as well. Naomi heard that life had improved in Bethlehem, and she decided to return. She asked her daughters-in-law to return to their own mothers and perhaps find new husbands, but they were reluctant to leave her. Finally Orpah returned to her home, but Ruth clung to Naomi, and said, "Where you go, I will go; Where you lodge, I will lodge; your people shall be my people, and your God my God."[15] Ruth had glimpsed something of God's love in her mother-in-law, and knew she must go with her.

The two women returned to Bethlehem, where Naomi told those who greeted her, "I went away full, but the LORD has brought me back empty."[16] referring to the loss of her menfolk. Naomi had even changed her name to refer to the bitterness she felt. In the patriarchal context of her life, she had yet to realize the treasure of devoted friendship she had brought with her. The two women had no home, no food, no future—only faith in God to support them. Ruth decided to glean in the barley field of Boaz (who was the son of Rahab), a wealthy kinsman of Naomi's husband. Boaz took note of Ruth's kindness to Naomi, offered her his protection, and told her he prayed that she would be rewarded by the God in whom she had come to trust.

Upon hearing of Boaz's kindness, Naomi developed a plan. Boaz planned to sleep on the threshing floor to celebrate the end of the harvest. Naomi instructed Ruth to go to the threshing floor after the food and drink and to sleep at the feet of Boaz, uncovering his lower body and waiting for him to tell her what to do. Ruth did so, and when Boaz awakened, Ruth asked him to spread his garment over her, for he was her next of kin. Boaz said he would do so because of her kindness, and he added that he would follow the levirate marriage law for the next of kin on her behalf. He suggested she stay until morning and leave when others would not see her, and he filled her veil with measures of barley. The next day Boaz agreed to marry Ruth and to redeem the land of Naomi's family. The townspeople who heard of this marriage called out blessings, among them this: "Through the children that the LORD will give you by this young woman, may your house be like the house of Perez, whom Tamar bore to Judah."[17]

Like Tamar and Rahab, Ruth was a foreigner. She was from the land of Moab, east of the Dead Sea, and her people were descendants of Lot. She came from the East, as did Abraham, and like him had left everything to start anew. Yet unlike him she had ventured into a strange land with no promise from God to guide her; she was taking initiative in a man's world, and taking care of an older woman as well. She had no help until she, with Naomi's guidance, acted on her own. Though it is less direct than with Tamar and Rahab, there is nonetheless a hint of daring sexual impropriety in the Book of Ruth. Under cover of nightfall, Ruth gambled on Boaz's honor and decency, and she won. But she took a significant risk, and could have lost. Yet the reader is given the distinct impression that she and Naomi would have found another way to survive.

No one knows exactly what took place on the threshing room floor because Ruth's actions, like her family's land and their ancestral line, were redeemed by Boaz. As a son of Rahab, Boaz probably respected independent and vulnerable women, and joined with Ruth in seeking to help the marginalized feminine, which both she and Naomi represented. What Boaz willingly did for Ruth was to follow the levirate marriage duty, the very thing that Judah refused to provide for Tamar. Ruth's youthful devotion brought healing and renewed relationship to the disparate parts of the family of Naomi and Boaz. When Ruth had a son, the women of the community were fully aware of the blessing that Ruth had brought, and they said to Naomi: "Blessed be the Lord, who has not left you this day without next-of-kin; and may his name be renowned in Israel! He shall be to you a restorer of life and a nourisher of your old age; for your daughter-in-law who loves you, who is more to you than seven sons, has borne him."[18]

Mary would have known the story of Ruth and how the young woman's fortunes fell and rose. She would have known how her faithfulness was eventually rewarded. But it was her devotion to an older woman and her readiness to follow the counsel of one that may have spoken most clearly to Mary. As Ruth turned to Naomi, so Mary turned to Elizabeth, and both young women found in the older women solace and affirmation, friendship and blessing.

BATHSHEBA

The first three female ancestors were agents of change in their own lives and the lives of those around them, but the fourth, Bathsheba, was more passive, and only once exercised her initiative. Rather than being an actor in her life's story, she was more acted upon, and we see her through the eyes of others, primarily as an object of desire. Her story is told in several books of the Bible: 2 Samuel, chapters11–12; 1 Kings 1:11–21, 28–31, 2:13–21; and 1 Chronicles 3:5.

We see Bathsheba first through the eyes of King David, who, looking down from his roof, saw her bathing and asked who she was. Bathsheba was purifying herself after menstruating, taking the ritual bath, or *mikvah*. Menstrual blood was taboo because it was both powerful and life-giving, and it was believed to arouse a man's uncontrolled desire.[19] So from the beginning of her relationship with David, Bathsheba is explicitly connected to the female life force. Despite the fact that she was married to one of his soldiers, Uriah the Hittite, who was away battling for David's kingdom, David found Bathsheba's beauty irresistible, and he sent for her and took her to his bed. We learn nothing of how Bathsheba experienced the situation, whether she was frightened and coerced, objected and struggled, or was flattered and willing. Whatever the case, David clearly abused his power.

Shortly afterward Bathsheba notified David that she was pregnant. David summoned Uriah the Hittite home, ostensibly to learn how the war was going, but in reality so that Uriah's time at home with his wife would cover David's infidelity. Uriah came, but because his men had no leave to be with their wives and because the army of Israel was consecrated to God, the honorable Uriah refused to spend the night with his wife, even though David went so far as to get him drunk. David then sent Uriah back to the fighting with sealed orders that instructed his superior to put him in the forefront of the battle. Consequently Uriah was killed, and after Bathsheba mourned for her husband, David made her his wife and she bore him the son of his adultery.

Again we are given no sense of Bathsheba's perspective. It may have been that she loved Uriah the Hittite. As a foreigner, he may have been more in touch with those who were marginalized and less powerful, such as women and children. Perhaps he was attuned to the dreams she had for her life. Perhaps theirs was a great and mutual love. We do not know if she was heartbroken, angry, resigned, or relieved, for it is David who is portrayed as the active person, the one with whom we are to identify. He, like Tamar, Rahab, and Ruth, was the trickster in the drama, but unlike the others, he failed in his trickery. He failed because there was no goodness, no divine end in his trickery. God was angry with David, and sent the prophet Nathan to confront him with a clever story of a man who, although he had many flocks, took the one beloved ewe lamb of another. David was incensed and judged the man harshly. Then Nathan informed David that David himself was that man, and the prophet pronounced God's judgment: Strife would never leave David's kingdom, others would someday take his wives, and the child he had with Bathsheba would die. All of those judgments came to pass.

From that moment until the end of his life, David was changed. He had lost his fighting edge and could no longer rule effectively. He spent the next two decades daily repenting for his sins against God. On David's deathbed Nathan sent Bathsheba to inform the king of the treachery of Adonijah (his son by another wife), and to suggest that David put his second son, Solomon, on the throne. It was here and only here that Bathsheba joined the other three foremothers in taking initiative to influence history, but she differed in that she did so at the request of a man. However, it is important to note that the man was Nathan the prophet, and his request to her indicates the respect he had come to have for her. She made a persuasive case to the king, saying that if Solomon was not made king, both she and her son would be counted as offenders and their lives would be at risk.[20] She had been the most beloved of all David's wives, and as his love had continued long after her youth had gone, the dying king agreed and Solomon became king.

Of all the foremothers, Bathsheba is the one that lived closest to the locus of power in Israel. She was the wife of the greatest of kings, a king whose name became a point of pride for all his descendants. But because of his desire for her, that same king had turned treacherous, and Bathsheba had lost a husband and a child because of his sins. Even so, the house and lineage of David were significant ancestral ties from which the Messiah was to come. Jesus was recognized as coming from that line. Perhaps Mary saw in Bathsheba that the illustrious house of David was balanced with mourning as well as dancing.

SCANDAL

These four women ancestors remind us that when God became incarnate among us, he came not only via the main street, the chaste, upright, and married; but also by way of the back alley, through disgrace, trickery, and treason. Each of the foremothers stood in the difficult light of scandal, and each showed initiative to change the course of history. Their stories help us gain a fuller understanding of Mary, who stands in the same line. Her own pregnancy was tinged with scandal, and Matthew's inclusion of the other women ancestors in the genealogy challenges the often saccharine image of Mary by showing us four of the determined, hardscrabble, and godly women who share the Savior's lineage.

Some have thought that the scandal of Jesus' birth was even greater than Christianity has been willing to recognize. Near the end of the eighth chapter of John's gospel, Jesus engaged in a long conversation with his opponents. He spoke to them of truth and freedom, of honoring God and Abraham. At one point they countered, "We are not illegitimate children; we have one father, God himself."[21] Jesus was speaking of spiritual legitimacy, but his opponents countered with physical legitimacy. Some biblical scholars have seen this passage as evidence of an early tradition of the illegitimacy of Jesus. In the first century, Jesus, in Jewish literature, was referred to as Yeshu ben Pantiri, or Jesus, son of Pantera.[22] The pagan philosopher Celsus, writing in the second century A.D., postulated that Jesus was the son of a poor woman who had been raped or seduced by a Roman soldier named Pantera.[23] It has been suggested that the illegitimacy of Jesus was a hidden tradition in the New Testament, which was eventually masked by the more acceptable concept of the virgin birth.[24] Jesus is referred to in rabbinical literature of the fourth century as Jeshu ben Stata and Jeshu ben Pandira, and at least one scholar concludes that the names are relics of "ancient Jewish mockery against Jesus, the clue to whose meaning is now lost."[25]

The New Testament, however, does not give evidence that such a theory was abroad before the second century. Paul's letter to the Galatians says that Jesus was "born under the law."[26] An illegitimate birth would not have been considered lawful. But one phrase from the gospels has given rise to questioning the issue of illegitimacy: In Mark 6:3 Jesus is described as "the son of Mary." Elsewhere Jesus is described as "the son of Joseph" or "the son of the carpenter," and the use of the father's name was the usual appellation. Some scholars have suggested that the term in Mark 6:3 implies that Jesus was illegitimate, but there is no evidence that illegitimate children were known by their mothers' names in the Hebrew Bible or in Jewish literature of that time.[27] The remarks of Jesus' opponents in the Gospel of John clearly show challenges to Jesus on many fronts, not the least of which is his birth. Regardless of the way in which first-century skeptics, opponents of Jesus, or believers in him viewed the circumstances of the birth, we can well understand how Mary might have drawn courage and consolation from her son's foremothers and their stories.

TRADITION

Religious tradition is another way we formulate our personal theology, and the rich tradition of the Hebrew people was an avenue of theological understanding for Mary. She and Joseph practiced the observances of devout Jews. In addition to the Ten Commandments given at Sinai, there was a code of corollary principles that included 613 obligations.[28] As Mary fulfilled the obligations of the law and kept the prescribed feasts and fasts, her understanding of her relationship with God deepened. To be a practicing Jew was to practice daily prayer, and there were prayers for most occasions. She also followed the customary religious patterns for rites of passage.

Following her betrothal period, she and Joseph most likely were married in a ceremony prescribed in the Talmud, which contained features that remain in Jewish weddings today. The bride was carried in on a palanquin, veiled and ornamented with gold. The bridegroom formally released the bride from any vows she might have made prior to that day. They then exchanged vows beneath a nuptial canopy. The celebrant pronounced blessings over the couple, and then they drank from a cup of blessed wine. Then the groom put a ring on the bride and stated that she was consecrated to him. The celebrant took another cup of wine and then recited seven blessings over the couple, concluding with "Blessed art thou, O Lord, who makest the bridegroom to rejoice with the bride." Then the celebrant drank from the wine and the newlyweds did the same. The celebrant poured away what was left and broke the glass. The ceremony concluded with the recitation of Psalm 45, to be repeated for the next seven days at the home of the newlyweds.[29]

Mary and Joseph followed the tradition of having Jesus circumcised on the eighth day,[30] as prescribed by the covenant God made with Abraham.[31] Originally, circumcision was performed by the mother, but by the time of Jesus, a specialist, called a Mohel, performed the surgery. This was done in the presence of the parents and with a special chair set aside for Elijah, who was presumed to be present as herald of the Messiah. Some of the spoken blessings that are still in use date from the time of Jesus. At the conclusion the father of the child says, "Blessed art thou, O Lord our God, King of the universe, who has hallowed us by thy commandments, and has commanded us to make our sons enter into the covenant of Abraham our father." In response, the people attending answer, "Even as this child has entered into the covenant, so may he enter into the Torah, the nuptial canopy, and into good deeds."[32]

In the first century, the wound of circumcision was treated with cumin powder and a powdered bog myrtle, and then with oil and wine. It was dressed with fine linen and tied with a red string, which was to remain in place for eight days. Twenty-five days later, Mary was to take Jesus to the temple. On the prescribed day, Mary would have entered the temple through the Door of the Newly Born, which was on the east side. From the women's gallery, she probably could have seen the priest cut the throat of and burn one of the doves that she and Joseph had offered. From that moment her son had now entered the Jewish Covenant and its unique place in the presence of God.[33] Though she felt comfort and order in the traditions of her people, the Gospel of Luke tells of one incident that gave Mary new and disturbing understanding. As they took the infant Jesus to be presented in the temple, they met the ancient and prophetic Simeon, who took the child in his arms and exclaimed:

> Master, now you are dismissing your servant in peace,
> according to your word;
> for my eyes have seen your salvation,
> which you have prepared in the presence of all peoples,
> a light for revelation to the Gentiles
> and for glory to your people Israel.[34]

The Song of Simeon, or Nunc Dimittis, after the first words in Latin, foretells the outreach of the gospel, and for centuries has been a beloved canticle for evening prayer. But Simeon had even more alarming things to say to Mary alone:

> This child is destined for the falling and the rising of many in Is-
> rael, and to be a sign that will be opposed so that the inner
> thoughts of many will be revealed—and a sword will pierce your
> own soul too.[35]

These words presaged the political realities that would eventually culminate in the cross. How the young mother understood
them within the cultural context of taking the child to the temple
for the first time we will never know, but we can be sure that they
factored into the theology she was constructing. Simeon's words
had to be alarming. The word he used for sword, *romphaia*, means
a sword of great size, a serious weapon, something that would
cause a significant injury. That sword was given material form in
the lance that pierced Jesus at Calvary. Not only would Mary suffer as the person who knew Jesus the best and, we may assume,
loved him the most, but she also would suffer because Christ's
death would cause her to question God's purposes. The in-
scrutability of God's ways may have led her to doubt and even de-
spair. The sword that Simeon mentioned to Mary had many
manifestations. That is clearly depicted in Latino sculptures, or *san-
teros*, of Mary, which show her with many swords piercing her
breast. Her only shield was the shield of faith, the power of those
who put their trust in God.

Simeon was described as a righteous and devout man, one on
whom the Holy Spirit rested. He represented the Jewish tradition
from which Mary came. He was also a person steeped in the
prophets, especially the prophet Isaiah. Simeon's own prophecy
saw in the infant Jesus the suffering servant, the "man of sorrows."
From the first two servant songs, Isaiah 42:6 and 49:6, Simeon bor-
rows the phrase "a light to the nations." But his overall message
echoes the third and fourth servant songs: Isaiah 50:6 and 53:2–3.
Mary's son is the long-awaited Messiah king, the infant to whom
the Magi had brought tribute, but he is also the prophesied servant,
the one "acquainted with infirmity." Three weeks earlier Mary and
Joseph had asked God's blessing for their son's life. Now she was
being confronted with a new understanding of Jesus as the afflicted
one who will bear our sins.

REASON

The third avenue of theological understanding is reason. We are encouraged to use our God-given minds to understand our relationship with God. As any teacher or student knows, the route to reason, which is "the capacity for rational thought, inference, or discrimination,"[36] is best traveled by asking questions. Question and answer is the traditional format of a catechism, and "An Outline of the Faith" in the *Book of Common Prayer* retains that format. Mary asked questions. So confident was she with questions that she challenged the annunciating angel Gabriel, asking, "How can this be, since I am a virgin?"[37] She was not intimidated by the divine, and later probed the twelve-year-old Jesus after he had stayed behind at the temple in Jerusalem, "Child, why have you treated us like this?"[38] Mary was comfortable with the interrogative; she expected responses and received them. No doubt she asked many more questions during her life, but those two tell us something about the way she gathered information and interacted with the world.

Her questions give us a glimpse into the way she thought. We are often encouraged to put on "the mind of Christ," but we usually don't think about the mind of Mary and how she influenced the mind of Christ. An unusual painting in the Castle Museum, in Norwich, England, shows Mary deep in thought. It was painted by Alice Havers in the nineteenth century, and titled, "Mary kept all these things and pondered them in her heart." It is significant that the Bible uses the phrase "pondered them in her heart"; the Hebrew understanding of *heart* refers to the whole person, the intellect, will, emotions, and body. In today's parlance the word *heart* usually refers to the actual organ or to a sentimental, emotional feeling. The Jews of Mary's time had a much fuller view. When we think of Mary doing theology, it can be helpful to look at the Orthodox Church's understanding of the Prayer of the Heart.

This tradition, which arose in the fifth century, holds that although we first begin to pray with our lips and our intellect, if we persevere the intellect and heart become united, and the prayer is eventually offered with the whole being. Over time the prayer infuses the consciousness and gradually begins to say itself.[39] The Sufi branch of Islam considers the heart to be a source of wisdom, and sweetness and tenderness are valued as the fruits of wisdom and contemplation, not simply as pleasant personal qualities. The heart is seen as a place of sheltered contemplation where wisdom is born. The mystical Sufi poet Rumi described the heart as having an inner, eternal intelligence, which he contrasted with the acquired intelligence of the mind.[40]

When Mary, in the Magnificat, uses the phrase that we have translated as "the imagination of the heart," she is speaking of that center from which a person's sense of self derives. When a person gestures to indicate her or his own person, she or he usually gestures toward the chest, where the heart is; not the head, where the brain is. In fact, recent studies of heart transplant recipients indicate the possibility of cellular memory within the heart.[41] It is interesting, when we consider the possibility of the heart having some capacity for memory, that the closing blessing for Rite 1 in the *Book of Common Prayer* asks that God's peace would keep the congregation's "hearts and minds in the knowledge and love of God." This blessing first appeared in the 1548 prayer book, and implies an understanding of human memory that includes the heart as well as the mind or brain.[42]

In the Gospel of Luke, when we hear of the shepherds who rushed to find the Christ child, we are told: "All who heard it were amazed at what the shepherds told them. But Mary treasured all these words and pondered them in her heart."[43] Mary was aware of the continuity of divine intervention in the pregnancy and birth, and sought to comprehend God's purpose in her family life as it unfolded. The experience of Elizabeth, the shepherds, Simeon, and others confirmed her own experience, and she beheld the mystery of incarnation with ongoing interest and amazement. Later, when she experienced Jesus lost in the temple, she once again ruminated over the meaning of what had happened, as she "treasured all these things in her heart."[44]

Beverly Gaventa points out: "Mary does not wait passively for someone else to explain things to her; she takes an active part by thinking, reflecting, considering matters. Surely if the evangelists explained how John the Baptist or Peter pondered over Jesus, the church would long ago have dubbed these as moments of theological reflection. Because the reflecting subject is a woman, her pondering has been cast in sentimental and trivializing terms. Mary . . . is initiating Christian reflection."[45] As she tried to understand God's will in the child with whom she had been entrusted, this child who was God in human form, this child who would eventually suffer and die ignominiously, she was engaged in a new understanding of God, and in doing so, we can say she was the first Christian theologian.[46] Because pondering is a silent occupation, Mary's example reminds us that an acquired taste for silence aids the theological task, as does a questioning mind.

EXPERIENCE

Finally, we come to experience as a component of theology. Our own lives and histories provide us with understanding of how God works in history. How did Mary understand her experience in relation to her faith? Although we know the scripture Mary knew, the traditions she observed, and even something of how she would have understood her situation, we are more limited when we try to reconstruct her experience. In this area it is helpful to let Mary's own words speak to us. One key word that Mary used to describe herself was *servant*. She saw herself as "the servant of the Lord" from the servant people of Israel. The King James Version uses the term *handmaid*. Though it sounds less lowly, it still means a servant, a slave. Despite the high office to which Mary had been called, she still continued to identify with the poor. The Greek word for servant, *doulos*, meant "slave" in a time and place where bondage and forced labor were common. The Hebrews accepted the social evil of slavery, but they required that slaves be set free after seven years. And they brought slaves into their covenant with God, circumcised them, and allowed them to observe the Sabbath.

Consequently, the term *slave* was a flexible one because a slave had mobility. He or she could be considered a vital member of the household, and so the word could also be synonymous with *child*. The term was rich with nuance, and Mary used it with the understanding that the one she served was God and that the shackle of the bondage was love. She was a "slave," "servant," and "child" of God, and that is how she defined her vocation. It is important to recognize that Jesus, like his mother, saw servanthood as crucial to his theology. He began his ministry by reading the first song of the servant from Isaiah,[47] and when he said, "I am among you as one who serves,"[48] it was clear that servanthood also formed his understanding of his vocation.

Much has been said of Mary's consent when the angel visited her. "Let it be with me according to your word" summarizes her theological understanding. It is similar to the words Jesus taught in the Lord's Prayer, "Your will be done,"[49] and it is echoed in his acceptance of the cross. Although the cross is the supreme example of self-giving and obedience, the Annunciation is also an example of obedience. But it is important to look at the nature of obedience, because Mary's obedience has at times been mistakenly understood as passivity. Obedience that flies in the face of convention and aligns itself with God rather than social norms is a radical and free act. Her obedience was of an order higher than others understood. She followed her inviolate soul, and trusted that her life could have meaning in God's plan. As Jaroslav Pelikan points out, "Obedience that is open to the future should be defined as supreme activity, not passivity."[50] Could Mary have taught the young Jesus active obedience? Could she have conveyed to her child how a person lives out her or his faith? In more than one sense, Jesus was the fruit of Mary's experience of God.

Did Mary share with her young son her experience of how God had acted in her history? Did she tell him of her vocation, of how she understood herself as the servant of God? Could her story have helped him understand the full nature of his mission? We do not know for sure, but it seems reasonable to assume that she did. In our next chapter, we will explore Mary's unique journey of discipleship and see more clearly the day-to-day struggles she had while following her son. The path was not easy, but Jesus never denigrated women, nor did he discourage their theological thinking. And when asked to judge the merits of two women, one who was doing housework and cooking, and the other who was listening to religious teaching, he chose the latter,[51] thereby forever encouraging the spiritual and theological training of women and all vocations that spring from such study.

A no-nonsense deacon friend told me that she had always been interested in Mary. She had felt called to serve God and had gone to seminary before the ordination of women, and because there were only two women in her class, at times had felt very lonely. She remembered standing in a congregation feeling alone and alienated from the church, and then a surprising and palpable sense of Mary's presence came over her. She said it felt like a friend was standing beside her. She realized then how much Mary had been through, how much she had suffered, and my friend said that she felt both Mary's strength and her friendship. It occurred to her that Mary was there, supporting her in her studies and in her vocation to serve and minister. Perhaps something of the vocation of Mary has been with all women who have sought deeper theological understanding, not simply the few who have felt her presence.

QUESTIONS FOR STUDY, PRAYER, AND REFLECTION

1. Which of the four female ancestors of Jesus speaks most to you? Why? If each of the foremothers in Matthew's genealogy gave Jesus something of her own nature, how do you think their influence was manifested in his life?

2. Is there an ancestor in your life with whom you particularly resonate? Who and why? Does that person's life help you to better understand yours?

3. As you look at images of Mary, do any in particular lead you to see her as a theologian? What does a theologian look like? Has your theology evolved by pondering things in your heart? If so, when and where has this happened?

4. Mary used the word *servant* to describe her understanding of her relationship with God. Which word would you use to describe your relationship with God?

5. In your faith journey, how have scripture, tradition, reason, and experience led and supported you? Which has been the most important?

5 &⋆ As Disciple

All these were constantly devoting themselves to prayer, together with certain women, including Mary the mother of Jesus, as well as his brothers. (Acts: 1:14)

The Anointing of Jesus
(Adapted from Luke 7:36–50)

"a woman of the city, who was a sinner," speaks

Tears

I have my grandmother's bottle for tears.
It's made of blue glass with a long twisted throat.
The hollow holds what the eye volunteers
from onions or mourning, heartbreak or mote.
I can still see her black eyes, shining and wet,
but I don't need reserve for this evening's task.
New tears are forming to honor a debt.
My sorrow, the liquid; this body, the flask.

I'll use them to wash the feet of the guest
whose words have invited me into God's reign.
While most rabbis treat me as vermin or jest,
his teaching renders joy for my pain.
Grandmother thought tears could make deserts bloom.
I feel a blossoming inside this room.

Discipleship

In addition to being named the first Christian theologian, Mary has been called the first Christian disciple. A disciple is a pupil of a teacher whose views and practices he or she is learning or taking on. As a disciple Mary first followed the word of God as she received it from the angel Gabriel, and then raised the child she had been given. Gradually the give-and-take of teaching and learning that comprises the parent-child relationship led to a role reversal, and eventually Mary began to follow Jesus as his disciple. In the New Testament, disciples followed groups such as the Pharisees, and individuals such as John the Baptist, as well as Jesus.

Many have viewed the disciples of Jesus as only the twelve men that Jesus called, but the term can be applied rightly to all those who followed Jesus, including women and children. We see the implied inclusion of women most clearly in the Gospel of Luke. In Galilee Jesus is accompanied by "a great crowd of his disciples,"[1] and when he enters Jerusalem, "the whole multitude of the disciples"[2] is with him. When Jesus sends out the seventy as well as the twelve, there is no indication that the seventy were all men.[3] When the two angels at the empty tomb urge the women to recall Jesus' words, saying, "Remember how he told you, while he was still in Galilee, that the Son of Man must be handed over to sinners, and be crucified, and on the third day rise again,"[4] they are referring to words spoken to "only the disciples,"[5] which clearly indicates that the women were considered to be among the disciples. For Mary, as for all the followers of Jesus, discipleship included taking on the discipline of loving one's neighbor and forgiving one's enemies. But her case was unique, and to follow her son meant a great amount of intellectual, psychological, emotional, and spiritual growth and development as well.

Discipline, with its inherent challenges and rewards, is part of the Christian journey. Sometimes we are unaware of the discipline of others until we are confronted with it. A faithful member of her church, my grandmother, in her nineties and on a small and fixed income, still attempted to tithe. My mother was concerned because she didn't want her mother to go without heat in the winter, and she asked me, on one visit, to speak to the minister and apprise him of my grandmother's financial situation. I did so, and the minister kindly visited my grandmother and tried to help her lower her contribution. My grandmother was indignant and insisted on her tithe. That was who she was. That was her discipline, and she was not pleased with anyone who would suggest that she do otherwise. She reasoned that the true disciple accepts the discipline.

Mary's own path of discipleship was particularly complex. She went from being Jesus' first teacher and the one he followed as a child, to accepting him as her teacher and following him. The gospels give us hints of how she juggled her role with her son and some of the stresses along the way. Upheaval was not unknown to Mary, and her life was often neither peaceful nor comfortable. Politics disrupted any comfort in her pregnancy when, close to her delivery date, the Roman emperor decreed that all people should be registered for tax purposes. Accompanying Joseph, Mary had to undertake the considerable journey from Nazareth to Bethlehem because her husband was descended from the house of David, and Bethlehem is the city of David:

> He went to be registered with Mary, to whom he was engaged and who was expecting a child. While they were there, the time came for her to deliver her child. And she gave birth to her first-born son and wrapped him in bands of cloth, and laid him in a manger, because there was no place for them in the inn.[6]

The Gospel of Matthew heightens the tension of the birth narrative with the story of the Magi and their brush with the political intrigue of Herod, who plots to use the travelers to discover potential insurgency among the Jews:

> On entering the house, they saw the child with Mary his mother; and they knelt down and paid him homage. Then, opening their treasure chests, they offered him gifts of gold, frankincense, and myrrh. And having been warned in a dream not to return to Herod, they left for their own country by another road.[7]

Those first pilgrims, the Magi, in an experience not unlike that of some contemporary pilgrims, found themselves caught unwittingly in a situation caused by political machinations. And Mary's vulnerability was suddenly of another order; no longer public scandal, now she was the focus of Herod's murderous and genocidal plot. Though secular history does not document the Slaughter of the Innocents, it does document Herod's ruthlessness. He is known to have killed forty-five Jewish leaders for resisting his occupation.[8] And the Proevangelium of James claims that Zechariah, Elizabeth's husband, was among those killed by Herod's soldiers as they searched for the infant messiah.

Peter Daino writes: "The massacre of the Bethlehem innocents, I believe, was the crucible event in which Mary's faith was forged. 'Whom shall my grief serve?' became the axial question around which Mary's life revolved. Indeed, this was the axial question on which the redemption of the whole world revolved. Would she succumb to bitterness and apostasy? Or would she be a spiritual mentor to Jesus, guiding him through apostolic grief to divine courage?"[9] Surely the slaughter of newborns, for a new mother, would have been a particularly significant and shattering event.

Now after they had left, an angel of the Lord appeared to Joseph in a dream and said, "Get up, take the child and his mother, and flee to Egypt, and remain there until I tell you; for Herod is about to search for the child, to destroy him." Then Joseph got up, took the child and his mother by night, and went to Egypt, and remained there until the death of Herod.[10]

In these passages from Matthew, Mary and the child are viewed through Joseph's eyes. Mary is his charge, and he is guided by his dreams on how to best protect her and her child. After the flight to Egypt and the massacre of the children, enough time passes for them to safely return.

When Herod died, an angel of the Lord suddenly appeared in a dream to Joseph in Egypt and said, "Get up, take the child and his mother, and go to the land of Israel, for those who were seeking the child's life are dead." Then Joseph got up, took the child and his mother, and went to the 'and of Israel.[11]

We see that the tension and danger of the infancy narrative of Matthew are relieved only by divine intervention. Mary's pregnancy out of wedlock initially could have meant exposure, humiliation, and even death, but Joseph responded to God's message. Joseph's openness to God's messages in his dreams meant that he perceived Herod's wholesale slaughter of infants in advance, and so was able to get his family to safety. But it also meant that they became refugees, traveling by night into a foreign land. Mary spent her early years with her child away from her village, her family, and friends. She was in a foreign culture with alien gods, different customs, and strange speech. Her one link with her past was Joseph. His attention to his dreams shows he was a sensitive and intuitive man, and it is reasonable to assume that their love and commitment grew in Egypt, as the child did in wisdom and stature.

JESUS AS AN ADOLESCENT

After the infancy narratives, the gospels pick up again when Jesus was twelve. Luke tells us that the Holy Family made annual trips to Jerusalem for the high holy days and to fulfill the law in Deuteronomy,[12] which prescribed three yearly pilgrimages to Jerusalem for males. Luke recounts one trip in particular that concerned Jesus:

> Now every year his parents went to Jerusalem for the festival of the Passover. And when he was twelve years old, they went up as usual for the festival. When the festival was ended and they started to return, the boy Jesus stayed behind in Jerusalem, but his parents did not know it. Assuming that he was in the group of travelers, they went a day's journey. Then they started to look for him among their relatives and friends. When they did not find him, they returned to Jerusalem to search for him. After three days they found him in the temple, sitting among the teachers, listening to them and asking them questions. And all who heard him were amazed at his understanding and his answers. When his parents saw him they were astonished; and his mother said to him, "Child, why have you treated us like this? Look, your father and I have been searching for you in great anxiety." He said to them, "Why were you searching for me? Did you not know that I must be in my Father's house?" But they did not understand what he said to them. Then he went down with them and came to Nazareth, and was obedient to them. His mother treasured all these things in her heart.[13]

In this passage we see the anxious mother of an adolescent asking plainly for an explanation. Any parent knows immediately the stress of a lost child. No doubt the first century also had its human predators. On finding him, when Mary told Jesus that she and his father had been searching in great anxiety, Jesus' response assumed that they understood his purpose, and this further confused Mary and Joseph. Some consider it odd that Mary was perplexed by Jesus' response, given the Annunciation and the miraculous things surrounding the birth; surely she knew this was an unusual child with special connections to the worship life of the community. And yet it is also clear that this was unusual behavior for Jesus.

The age of twelve is significant in this account because that is the time a Jewish boy assumes the first responsibilities toward manhood, the obligations of the law.[14] It is reasonable to assume that Jesus would have been informed at that time of the miraculous circumstances of his birth, and that he was the one on whom all of Israel's hopes depended. In that light his prolonged visit at his "Father's house" makes much more sense. And likewise we might better understand Mary's perplexity if we reflect on the influence of twelve years of child rearing, the daily routines and habitual ways of doing things, all of which can cloud the initial vision. This is also the place in scripture where the challenge of Mary's discipleship first becomes apparent.

The infancy narrative of Thomas tells a parallel story to that of Luke, but adds to it, giving to the Pharisees some of the words that Luke had earlier ascribed to Elizabeth:

> His mother Mary came up and said to him, "Child, why have you done this to us? Don't you see, we've been worried sick looking for you?" "Why are you looking for me?" Jesus said to them. "Don't you know I have to be in my father's house?" Then the scholars and the Pharisees said, "Are you the mother of this child?" She said, "I am." And they said to her, "You more than any woman are to be congratulated, for God has blessed the fruit of your womb! For we've never seen nor heard such glory and such virtue and wisdom." Jesus got up and went with his mother, and was obedient to his parents. His mother took careful note of all that had happened. And Jesus continued to excel in learning and gain respect.[15]

Scripture does not tell us much more about the incident. But it is possible that his parents came to understand the incident as formative in Jesus' understanding of his own vocation. For pilgrims, traveling to Jerusalem during high holy days was a time of joy. There was a party atmosphere, and it was exciting to be a part of it. It was also exciting for the boy to be growing up and taking part as a young adult. Parents of adolescents who remember their own adolescence know that many wonderful and mysterious processes are shaping the character, dreams, future, and personality of their child. Once parental fear is assuaged, they can see the child with tenderness and can nurture the new and exciting experiences out of which the future man or woman is being born. But there is also loss, the loss of the small child as he or she emerges into adulthood, and in Mary's case, the beginning of a distancing as her son clearly looked more and more to God and less and less to his parents. It is significant that Jesus chose to refer to God as *Abba,* which is actually better translated as "Daddy" than "Father." This choice may have been made to describe the closeness he had with God, vis-à-vis his relationship with his parents, and it also may have served to keep them at arm's length.

Growing with the child Jesus from infancy through childhood and into the teenage years, we may assume that there were moments of conflict between Mary and her son. Max Ernst painted a surprising and somewhat alarming picture of Mary spanking the Christ child. Although we don't often think of Mary as the mother of a difficult child, the incident in the temple resonates with many anxious parents. Luke has taken us from images of the serene Madonna to that of a stressed mother. Yet Jesus was more than her child; he was also the promised one, and she did not understand him. We can only begin to imagine her struggle. As Saint Augustine said, "What you fully understand cannot be God."[16] After the incident at the temple, the gospels are again silent about the youth of Jesus. We do not meet him again until he is baptized at about the age of thirty and begins his ministry.

CHALLENGES

Being the parent of the adult Jesus likewise had its challenges. His behavior and responses to his mother were at times disturbing and unorthodox. In the Gospel of Mark, the earliest of the gospels and the one with no birth narrative, Mark begins with the adult life of Jesus, and his gospel includes two references to Mary. After being in Galilee, Jesus returned to his home, "and the crowd came together again, so that they could not even eat. When his family heard it, they went out to restrain him, for people were saying, 'He has gone out of his mind.'" [17] Jesus' family tried to inhibit him because people were saying he had a demon or was insane. We do not have to read too far between the lines to feel the family tension. Following an encounter with the scribes, who also claimed that Jesus had an "unclean spirit," the gospel continues:

> Then his mother and his brothers came; and standing outside, they sent to him and called him. A crowd was sitting around him; and they said to him, "Your mother and your brothers and sisters are outside, asking for you." And he replied, "Who are my mother and my brothers?" And looking at those who sat around him, he said, "Here are my mother and my brothers! Whoever does the will of God is my brother and sister and mother." [18]

This story is repeated with slight variation in both Matthew and Luke. It clearly is a story of a family working at cross-purposes with Jesus, its perplexing and popular member. He was a conundrum, and they did not understand his purposes. His mother and his siblings may have been concerned for his safety because powerful forces were taking note of him, and Jesus seemed unaware of the danger. Or they may have begun to share the view that he was losing his mind, and they wanted to take him home and care for him. In any event Jesus did not cooperate with them. While his response to the announcement that his family was asking for him may initially seem dismissive of Mary and the rest of his family, Jesus used the opportunity to teach about the reign of God. The lesson was as pertinent for his mother and siblings as it was for the others. Jesus was consistently unconventional about family ties, and kept trying to enlarge our understanding of our connection to others. Some have viewed Jesus' words "Whoever does the will of

God is my brother and sister and mother" as actually honoring Mary, because she was one who clearly did the will of God, especially when she responded at the Annunciation, "Let it be with me according to your word." It seems more likely that if Jesus' words did refer to Mary, he meant them more as a pointed reminder that a familial relationship conveyed no special privileges and that his family had no particular right to interfere with his work.

Another passage shows again the tension within the family:

> On the sabbath he began to teach in the synagogue, and many who heard him were astounded. They said, "Where did this man get all this? What is this wisdom that has been given to him? What deeds of power are being done by his hands! Is not this the carpenter, the son of Mary and brother of James and Joses and Judas and Simon, and are not his sisters here with us?" And they took offense at him. Then Jesus said to them, "Prophets are not without honor, except in their hometown, and among their own kin, and in their own house." And he could do no deed of power there.[19]

Matthew tells a similar version of this story. Together, these stories demonstrate that Jesus was not understood by the townspeople, nor by members of his own household and that their lack of understanding hindered his work. Human family dynamics played out in his home as they do in others around the world. Familial stress is apparent in other gospel stories. Elsewhere in Matthew's gospel Jesus says:

> Do not think that I have come to bring peace to the earth; I have not come to bring peace, but a sword.
> For I have come to set a man against his father,
> and a daughter against her mother,
> and a daughter-in-law against her mother-in-law;
> and one's foes will be members of one's own household.
> Whoever loves father or mother more than me is not worthy of me; and whoever loves son or daughter more than me is not worthy of me.[20]

This story is repeated in Luke's gospel, and we see that a persistent theme of Jesus' is the inherent challenge that family life brings to the life of faith. It is in the nature of familial life to maintain the status quo. Jesus asked his followers to embark on a life of radical trust in God. Family ties would, quite simply, hold a person back.

A particularly pointed remark of Jesus' is related in the Gospel of Luke. "A woman in the crowd raised her voice and said to him, 'Blessed is the womb that bore you and the breasts that nursed you!' But he said, 'Blessed rather are those who hear the word of God and obey it.'"[21] Mary must have realized that Jesus was writing a new chapter in the relationship of God with human beings. The nuclear family was being exploded to enlarge the human family, and her status as mother and matriarch was being radically challenged and transformed. In effect, Jesus was saying that Mary was more blessed bearing God's word in her soul than in her body. How she synthesized and processed his responses, we will never know, but we can chart something of her zigzag course to understanding. We see a very human Mary in those scenes, no doubt baffled and bewildered by her son and struggling to comprehend what God was asking of her.

We can assume that during those times, Mary was evolving in her discipleship. The gospel stories show us that the family was far from modeling discipleship as Jesus understood it, and that the family eventually came a great distance in its transformation. This transformation included not only Mary but Jesus' brothers and sisters as well. Among his brothers was James, a strong leader in the early church and traditionally believed to have been the first bishop of the church in Jerusalem,[22] and Jude, a skilled exegete of the early church in Palestine and believed by most scholars to be the author of the Epistle of Jude.[23] But the transformation was apparently a slow one. Mary and the siblings of Jesus were not unlike the twelve named male disciples, in that they usually failed to understand Jesus and his purpose among them. And Mary's struggle was compounded by years of familial closeness and cultural expectations. She had to move in her understanding from worshiping a transcendent God to following and learning from a very immanent God, whom she had raised from infancy. Jesus' siblings also would have had complicated faith journeys. That is clear even if we factor in only sibling rivalry. The eventual titles given to Jesus, which were in use in the circles of his family, include Messiah, Lord or Our Lord, and Master.[24] The family followed Jesus as he engaged in his increasingly unorthodox teaching, developed his worrisome popularity, suffered his public humiliation and death, and finally attained his Resurrection. We should not assume that it was easy.

Mary had been hailed as "full of grace" by the annunciating angel. The years that followed that Annunciation would tax and vex her, and yet she followed Jesus and changed as his teaching called her to do. The theologian Dietrich Bonhoeffer developed the idea of cheap grace in his book *The Cost of Discipleship*. Cheap grace is that which does not challenge us or ask us to change; rather, it claims to grant us the blessings of the Christian life without insisting that we follow Christ. It secularizes the faith and deceives those who would be faithful. Bonhoeffer contrasts cheap grace with costly grace, which is "costly" because it asks everything of us, and "grace" because the only full and true life is a gift. He says we must renounce a self-willed life and assent to the discipline of following Christ.[25] Despite the difficulties God's grace was sufficient for Mary. She assented to obedience, and eventually was able to look beyond the confusing child to behold the commanding God.

After reading the synoptic gospels, some might feel that Mary got more than her share of difficulties with Jesus. She clearly was faced with unique challenges, and maternal privileges were not accorded to her in Jesus' public ministry. A contemporary joke illustrates this: The scene is Jesus addressing the crowd around the woman caught in adultery. Jesus says, "Let anyone among you who is without sin be the first to throw a stone."[26] Then catching a glimpse of his mother winding up like a baseball pitcher, he says, "Aw, Mom . . ." Mary had to learn to understand herself and her role with Jesus differently. There was much work, much growth, and many changes to undergo. For her to adhere insistently to her status as mother and expect special consideration would have been for her to miss the point, and the word for sin in the New Testament literally means to miss the mark or miss the point.

Mary's challenges were not confined to the synoptic gospels. Two significant moments involve Mary and Jesus in the Gospel of John, and both are moments of transition. The first is the wedding at Cana, at which Mary indicated a direction that Jesus followed. The second significant exchange was at the cross. Jesus' hour had finally come, and his tone with his mother was very different:

Meanwhile, standing near the cross of Jesus were his mother, and his mother's sister, Mary the wife of Clopas, and Mary Magdalene. When Jesus saw his mother and the disciple whom he loved standing beside her, he said to his mother, "Woman, here is your son." Then he said to the disciple, "Here is your mother." And from that hour the disciple took her into his own home."[27]

Some commentators have viewed this exchange as the birth of the church, with Mary and the beloved disciple as the first of that new community, a community marked by mutual care.[28]

The exchange at the cross can be perplexing because even there Jesus was teaching. Its great tenderness is apparent only if we have begun to internalize Jesus' understanding of family as reaching beyond bloodlines. A brief story from the film *Gandhi* teaches the same lesson. It takes place when Gandhi was fasting to stop the violence between Hindus and Muslims in India. Very weak and near the point of death, he is approached by a Hindu man who is terribly agitated and says he is in hell because he has killed a child. He has killed a Muslim child in revenge for the death of his own child. The man is violent, almost crazed with grief and rage. He looks like one who is in hell. Gandhi's response is to say that he knows a way out of hell. He tells the man to find a child, another Muslim child, one whose parents are dead, and to adopt that child as his own, but to be sure to raise that child as a Muslim. Gandhi saw that beneath the rage and agitation were the hurt and longing of a parent who had lost a child. He also saw the deep danger of possessiveness, whether it is of one's children, one's cultural perspective, or one's religious tradition.

Jesus kept trying to tell us that we are all one family with one loving heavenly parent, and that we belong to one another. He wanted us to look beyond the limits of our biological family, our tribe, our ethnicity, our class, our religion. From the pain of the cross, he urged his mother to behold her new son and his disciple to behold his new mother. Let's take a moment and look at the disciple that Jesus chose to replace him as a child to Mary. Who was the disciple Jesus loved? Contemporary scholarship points to a younger disciple, and suggests one who had followed John the Baptist, not one of the twelve men Jesus named. Some have even suggested that the beloved disciple may have been a woman. That would provide an interesting corollary to Jesus' unorthodox views of family.

Christianity is a school of love, and it stretches the natural affections, even that most celebrated one between mother and child (the one the prophet Isaiah says is close to but not as abiding as God's love for us). But even at the cross, we do well to remember that Jesus learned his first lessons in that school of love at home. And as love begets love, Jesus' words from the cross demonstrate the reality of his bond with his mother, the sharing of genuine joys and sorrows and the shouldering of responsibility that love calls forth.

TO FOLLOW TO THE END

Mary at Golgotha has been especially helpful to those who are grieving, and the image of her at the foot of the cross has resonated with the bereaved down the centuries. In choosing Mary, God must have chosen a strong woman, because a lesser woman would have turned in rage from the cross. But this was a woman who did not demur from asking questions of God. We can assume that her most insistent and most impassioned queries were on Good Friday: Why did this happen? What could she have done differently? And yet she knew that even as she had tried to redirect Jesus, it had not made any difference. His path had been clearly chosen, and he would not allow himself to be guided otherwise. It was at Calvary that Mary's discipleship was reaching its apex, and she was learning in the core of her being that God's ways were not hers. We hear in Jesus' words from the cross that he had begun to care for and comfort the creature that had cared for and comforted him. In the "Paradiso," Dante's final canto begins, "Virgin mother, daughter of thy son."[29] She was learning at the feet of her master as she stood at the foot of the cross. And yet there still were no answers for her questions. The messiah promised to her by Gabriel had died like a common criminal.

While Jesus expressed concern that his mother have a son, it is worthy of note that another relative was with her at the Crucifixion. The Gospel of John includes others at the foot of the cross, and Mary's sister is listed among them. She is also named Mary, and designated Mary of Clopas, which may mean that she was Mary's sister, but more probably was her half-sister, sister-in-law, stepsister, or some other family relation for which modern English does not use the term *sister*.

We know from the early church historian Hegesippus that the person who succeeded Jesus' brother James as leader of the church in Jerusalem was Simon, son of Clopas. Clopas was the brother of Jesus' legal father, Joseph. (Some have viewed Clopas as the person named Cleopas, who met the risen Lord on the road to Emmaus in the Gospel of Luke.)[30] It is most likely, then, that Mary of Clopas was Mary the wife of Clopas, which would make her Mary's relative, and the term *sister* might most easily explain the relationship of Jesus' mother's husband's brother's wife.[31] In any case we can imagine a loving female relative and follower of Jesus supporting Mary as they stood appalled before the executions. From this brief but significant reference, we might assume that this particular relative of Mary's had been a support over the years.

Both women were also faithful disciples, in contrast to the male disciples who had betrayed Jesus, fled, or both. The other three gospels also say that women stood by Jesus at the cross, but while the name Mary is given, it is not always clear who the ones named Mary were. However, one Mary was clearly identified, and that was Mary Magdalene. She had followed Jesus since he had released her from spiritual and psychological torments, and she went on to be the first to see the risen Lord. Tradition has often viewed her as a reformed prostitute, but nothing in scripture leads to that conclusion. We know she was a woman who used her wealth to provide for Jesus and the disciples, and she was a devout follower of Jesus'. Mary Magdalene is listed as being at the cross in the gospels of Mark, Matthew, and John. Hers is the most consistent name, and we can assume there was a bond between her and Jesus' mother, if not before the cross, then certainly after.

WHO WENT TO THE TOMB?

Mary Magdalene is listed in Matthew, Mark, and John's gospels as one who went to the tomb and found it empty. Was Mary the mother of Jesus also one of those who went to the tomb on the first Easter morning? The earliest form of medieval theater that we know has three women named Mary come to the tomb, where they are asked, "Whom are you seeking?" "*Quem queritas?*" In parallel to the three Magi seeking the Christ child and carrying their offerings, these women come in search of Jesus with their oils and spices.[32] While they are named simply the three Marys, a recent adaptation of this scene as part of a medieval passion play performed at Stanford University interpreted one to be the mother of Jesus.[33] A contemporary Orthodox icon based on a similar one from the eighth century shows Mary with the angel at the empty tomb.[34] Similarly, a 1906 stained-glass window by Tiffany Studios shows two women meeting the angel at the site of the Resurrection. One, with long, curled reddish-blond hair looks much as Mary Magdalene has been depicted down the ages. The other, with her head and body covered in blue, looks very much like a traditional portrait of Mary the mother of Jesus.[35] Why do different artists spanning the centuries include Mary among the women at the tomb?

An obvious answer is that it is usually the family that performs the last sad duties of preparing the body for burial. In the time of Jesus, the task was to take spices, such as myrrh, cinnamon, and cassia, to anoint the body. But after the Crucifixion, there is no mention of Mary in the gospel accounts. She is not mentioned again until the event of Pentecost, chronicled in the Acts of the Apostles. Or is there another possible mention? The Gospel of Mark reads, following the Crucifixion, "There were also women looking on from a distance; among them were Mary Magdalene, and Mary the mother of James the younger and of Joses, and Salome. These used to follow him and provided for him when he was in Galilee; and there were many other women who had come up with him to Jerusalem."[36] Similarly, after Jesus is laid in the tomb of Joseph of Arimathea, the Gospel of Mark continues: "Mary Magdalene and Mary the mother of Joses saw where the body was laid. When the sabbath was over, Mary Magdalene, and Mary the mother of James, and Salome bought spices, so that they might go and anoint him."[37] These were the women who encountered the angel who told them that Jesus had risen.

Who were the women named Mary who encountered the angel at the empty tomb? Was the mother of Joses also the mother of James in the second passage? Was James the younger the same person as just plain James? Earlier, in the Gospel of Mark, the brothers of Jesus had been named as James, Joses, Judas, and Simon.[38] Could this woman, "the mother of James the younger and of Joses," have been Mary the mother of Jesus? This identification seemed plausible to some writers in the early church.[39] It has been suggested that Mary the mother of Jesus was also "Mary the mother of James," and to further complicate things, that she was also the mother of Salome.[40] If so, why wasn't she identified as the mother of Jesus? Could it have been that the names of the other children were used above the name of Jesus because they were still living, or perhaps, as has been suggested, because the evangelist Mark perceived Mary as an unbeliever?[41] A variant reading of Mark refers to "Mary (the wife) of James and Mary the mother of Jesus" as those who approached the tomb.[42]

The Gospel of Matthew gives a similarly cryptic account: At the cross the women who looked on from a distance were named "Mary Magdalene, and Mary the mother of James and Joseph, and the mother of the sons of Zebedee."[43] James and John were among the first disciples, and were known as the sons of Zebedee. James the son of Alphaeus, traditionally known as James the Less, to distinguish him from the son of Zebedee, was another of the disciples.[44] He may also have been "James the younger." But did he have a brother named Joseph or Joses? The Gospel of Matthew continues, "After the sabbath, as the first day of the week was dawning, Mary Magdalene and the other Mary went to see the tomb."[45]

Women named Mary appear to be everywhere. Like the name James, there are almost too many to assimilate. It is confusing and difficult to unravel the many strands. It has been suggested that the obfuscation could be deliberate, to marginalize the human family of Jesus and downplay its participation in favor of the cosmic and risen Christ.[46] In this perplexing mix, how do we gain some clarity? Perhaps it would help to think of the context. Wouldn't a mother who had followed her son to the cross go and do the final work of anointing his body? Aren't the bodies of their children, even if grown, the particular concern of mothers? After having stayed at the cross, it is not likely that the tomb would have held horrors she could not bear. And just as Mary had received news from an angel at the beginning of Jesus' life, so it seems fitting that she would receive news from a similar source at the end.

There is another interesting possibility for the identity of one of the Marys. The early church attributed the names of Mary and Salome to the sisters of Jesus.[47] It is worth noting that, according to historians, those were the two most popular female names during that time period, so the likelihood of accuracy is fairly good. The names of the two sisters are not found often, but do appear in some second- and third-century writings, and some scholarship from these texts indicates a tradition that the three Marys were Mary the mother of Jesus; Mary the sister of Jesus; and Mary Magdalene the companion of Jesus.[48] The three Marys seen as mother, sister, and friend of our Lord give an appealing and comprehensible simplicity in naming those who visited the empty tomb. Furthermore, if Jesus' other sister was named Salome, and Salome was named in Mark's gospel as one who brought spices to the tomb, it is reasonable to assume that it would have been the women of Jesus' family, his mother and sisters, who would complete the burial.

And yet it is also conceivable that the ordeal at the cross had exhausted and overwhelmed the mother of Jesus, and she was not among those who ventured to the tomb. She may have needed more than three days of rest, and her friends and extended family might have offered to perform the last sorrowful office at the grave for her. Many readers of scripture are satisfied with a number of different women named Mary, while others conclude that the many Marys noted are one and the same mother of Jesus.[49] Although we cannot be certain, it seems likely that Jesus' mother was among those named Mary who went to the tomb and one of the faithful women who first received news of the Resurrection, as artists clearly suggest.

One other named witness to the Resurrection was Joanna, who is named in the Gospel of Luke. Earlier she is mentioned as the wife of Herod's steward. Her husband would have been in charge of Herod's personal estate, and so would have had great standing in the community. Joanna had been cured by Jesus at the same time as Mary Magdalene,[50] and she was listed as one who went to the tomb and witnessed the risen Lord.[51] Thus we see that the Resurrection was a time when the female disciples in Jesus' life were visible and active. This provides another reason to assume that Mary was among them.

Other women are named in the gospels, but there are also many unnamed women whose gratitude for lives reordered out of chaos would have brought them to the circle of the disciples. There was the Syrophoenician woman whose daughter had been pulled back from madness, the woman with a hemorrhage who had been healed, the woman at the well to whom Jesus had told his purpose, and the woman who was designated as the great sinner in Luke's gospel. She had been an intuitive and expressive person, and had demonstrated great love and hospitality to Jesus by washing his feet with her tears and drying them with her hair. The poem that precedes this chapter reflects on her spiritual transformation through Jesus and the way she viewed her tears. Mary would have easily become the focus of gratitude for many of those whom Jesus had healed and taught.

APOSTLE

Though Mary was clearly a disciple, she was also an apostle, a term that in Greek means "one chosen and sent with a special commission as the fully authorized representative of the sender."[52] *Apostle* can refer to the twelve that Jesus chose, but it can refer also to those who witnessed the Resurrection and those who were present at Pentecost. Paul gained the title by experiencing the resurrected Jesus. It is a unique title, and one that cannot be passed on.

Paul used the word to include all who had received a commission from the risen Christ to preach the gospel. Among the apostles, Paul includes the brothers of Jesus, although they were generally known by the direct title "brothers of the Lord."[53] Mary, like her sons, had a stronger affiliation with Jesus than that of apostle, and yet her role in the Acts of the Apostles leads us to presume the title of *apostle* was easily hers as well.

It is worth noting the way in which Paul mentions the Lord's brothers in his epistle. That Paul includes Jesus' brothers when asking the church in Corinth if he did not have the right to food and drink, and to be accompanied by a wife as the other apostles did, suggests that the other apostles, including the brothers of Jesus, traveled with their wives. Paul's argument inadvertently gives us clues about Mary's later life: By including the brothers of Jesus in his letter, Paul suggests that the extended family of Jesus did not live celibate lives, and indeed that Mary's family circle probably was growing with grandchildren.

Of Mary's life after the cross, we know little except that she remained part of the community of disciples after the Resurrection, and so most probably encountered her resurrected son. We know from Paul's first letter to the Corinthians that the resurrected Lord made a special appearance to his brother James, and so it stands to reason that he also appeared to his mother. We are not given details of that meeting in scripture, but surely her joy would have been as large as her grief. We can imagine Mary's stunned and garbled words, her running and laughter and tears of joy. She had been on a long journey of understanding with her son, from the flight to Egypt to the streets of Nazareth, to Golgotha and then beyond the grave. She had followed—at times uncertain, at times concerned—but she had followed as a disciple, as the other women disciples who followed Jesus. And with the Resurrection, her understanding and faith had come full circle.

But still another experience of physical loss and new understanding awaited Mary. The Ascension of Jesus was the culmination of his time on Earth, but for his mother, it would present another challenge. Although Jesus promised to be with his followers forever, we can assume that she would have missed the familiarity of his person as she learned to trust in things unseen, unheard, and unknown. She had lost him twice before, and found him each time. The Ascension called her to a new level of faith and trust. We can imagine her standing among the disciples at the Ascension, sharing with them a longing for comprehension and a growing peace.

Even then Mary's work was not finished. We learn in the Acts of the Apostles that she was part of the early church community. After the Resurrection and Ascension, the remaining eleven disciples gathered to pray. Luke writes, "All these were constantly devoting themselves to prayer, together with certain women, including Mary the mother of Jesus, as well as his brothers."[54] We can certainly assume that she experienced Pentecost, the moment when the presence of God within the community came with an explosive intensity and new direction. Artistic depictions of the event down the ages show Mary as a central figure. She was a part of the young church that was energized, transformed, and comforted by that astonishing event, and which then began establishing a community of love and forgiveness within the violent and disjointed culture of the times.

The mention of Mary as part of the post-Ascension gathering in the Acts of the Apostles offers continuity by showing the immediate family, despite their initial slowness to understand, as part of the nucleus that would become the family of the church. It is clear that Mary had remained close to the other disciples and was an accepted and significant member of the beginning church. It is reasonable to think that her sister and her daughters joined with her and her sons in the new community. Mary would have offered the fledgling church her hard-won hope, faith, and charity, and she, who would later become known as the Blessed Mother, would fittingly become the spiritual mother of that community.

In the next chapter, we will explore Mary's role as it has moved from history and scripture into the religious life of the faithful. Let us leave the historical person of Mary with the image of her in that Pentecost community, among women and men who loved and respected her, a woman wakened to the astonishment of God's life among us. In the course of thirty-three years of stretched awareness and bewildered love, thirty-three years of birth pangs into a new reality, she came to fully grasp and convey the message of the one she had delivered in that stable. And through the cross and all that followed, she came to know that God, at even greater cost, had finally delivered her.

QUESTIONS FOR STUDY, PRAYER, AND REFLECTION

1. When Herod ordered the Slaughter of the Innocents, he followed a pattern that continues today. Reflect on women and children in modern war, and on civilian noncombatants in contemporary conflicts.

2. Name the stresses Mary faced as she struggled with discipleship. Are any of them your own?

3. True discipleship was described by the theologian Dietrich Bonhoeffer as "costly." What does following Jesus cost you?

4. If Jesus had sisters who followed him to the cross and beyond, brothers who served the church, and one who later became a leader in the Jerusalem church, how do you understand Jesus' words from the cross to his mother and the disciple he loved? How do you imagine his interactions with his sisters and his brothers?

5. In hymn 673 of the Episcopal Church hymnal, the third stanza reads: "The first ones ever, oh, ever to know of the rising of Jesus, his glory to be, were Mary, Joanna, and Magdalene, and blessed are they are they who see."[55] Reflect on these women. What do you think it was like for them to follow Jesus? Contrast Joanna with Nicodemus (John 3:1–10).

6 &. As Intercessor

"They have no wine." (John 2:3)

CANA

Because she must have known
how the glimmer in blue shadows
becomes the flight of swallows;

how the long limbs of moonlight
make mystery welcome;
how wonder is a kind of manna.

It was, after all, her idea.
She had seen the hour flagging.
Why else would she insist?

She knew how a moment turned back
with a halt or refusal
and all of life turned with it.

She knew also how eternity surfaced,
how light-reflecting water
could sweeten in our mouths to wine.

SOLACE

About ten years ago, in the north of England, I found myself standing in the ruins of Finchale Abbey, an ancient priory. My husband and daughter had gone to an amusement park, and I had gone with friends by bus to this site on the River Wear. My friends had wandered off, and a map of the ruins had helped me locate the stones that were once the Lady Chapel built by Saint Godric, an eleventh-century pirate-turned-hermit who lived at Finchale until well after his hundredth year. I had taken off my shoes and was standing to pray at the east end of the erstwhile chapel. I was not sure why I had sought out the chapel dedicated to Mary; devotion to Mary had not been part of my prayer life or spirituality, but I had wanted to find that space.

It was a sunny afternoon, and a few other tourists and holiday-makers were around. As I stood on the cool grass amid the gray stones and prayed for healing from the sadness of a miscarriage the year before, I was interrupted by a child's voice asking if I'd like to see something. I turned to see a seven-year-old local boy looking eagerly at me. Nonplussed, I said, "Yes," and he showed me a narrow tower with a tiny circular stair that he had found. I thanked him, but he wanted to show me more. He had also found a wine cellar. He obviously had been exploring.

I was a bit puzzled that he chose a middle-aged woman as a playmate. I asked if he was alone, and he pointed out his grandparents in the distance. We wandered together and talked, and soon I realized that the afternoon had flown and the last bus would be leaving shortly. I told the boy that I had wanted to say a prayer, and asked if he would like to join me. He said he thought he would because his mother had died just two weeks before.

We stood in our silent prayers, and then I got ready to leave. My friends met me, and I introduced them to my new companion. As we were getting ready to go, one of my friends took me aside and said she did not think the boy wanted me to go. So before going I asked him if he would like to stay in touch, to be pen pals. He said he would like that very much, and so we have remained friends, pen pals and e-mail pals, and we have visited whenever I am able to return to England. I did not realize for some time that my prayer for healing had been answered in the form of a child who had lost a mother, just as I had lost a child.

I did not know why I had felt drawn to the chapel dedicated to Mary, but throughout the centuries, many Christians have turned to Mary and asked for her intercession to aid their prayer at particularly difficult or sensitive times in their lives. Needs of the faithful have moved her from the confines of scripture to an active presence in religious and cultural life, with an understanding of her as both the mother of Christ and a spiritual mother of all Christians. But other Christians have maintained Mary solely as a historical personage, and are uncomfortable with what they perceive as lifting her to a significance dangerously close to that properly reserved for God.[1] Noted voices in the Anglican tradition have taken eloquently different points of view. George Herbert wrote a poem saying he would gladly turn to Mary if only Jesus had instructed him to do so. And John Keble, also through a poem, urged the faithful to address Mary with an "Ave" and directly ask for her intercession.[2] Though there is still bifurcation in the Anglican experience of Mary, this chapter will illustrate a gradual shift toward a middle ground.

A WOMAN CLOTHED WITH THE SUN

A basic Anglican understanding of Mary is to view her as a faithful disciple and companion in the Christian journey, but she is also understood as first among the saints. However, some have viewed her as having a cosmic dimension, an understanding that seems to derive from a vision described by John in Revelation:

> A great portent appeared in heaven: a woman clothed with the sun, with the moon under her feet, and on her head a crown of twelve stars. She was pregnant and was crying out in birth pangs, in the agony of giving birth. Then another portent appeared in heaven: a great red dragon, with seven heads and ten horns, and seven diadems on his heads. . . . Then the dragon stood before

the woman who was about to bear a child, so that he might devour her child as soon as it was born. And she gave birth to a son.
. . . But her child was snatched away and taken to God and to his throne; and the woman fled into the wilderness. . . .

And war broke out in heaven; Michael and his angels fought against the dragon. The dragon and his angels fought back, but they were defeated. . . . The great dragon was thrown down, that ancient serpent, who is called the Devil and Satan, the deceiver of the whole world—he was thrown down to the earth, and his angels were thrown down with him. . . .

So when the dragon saw that he had been thrown down to the earth, he pursued the woman who had given birth to the male child. But the woman was given the two wings of the great eagle, so that she could fly from the serpent into the wilderness, to her place where she is nourished for a time. . . . Then from his mouth the serpent poured water like a river after the woman, to sweep her away with the flood. But the earth came to the help of the woman; it opened its mouth and swallowed the river that the dragon had poured from its mouth. Then the dragon was angry with the woman, and went off to make war on the rest of her children, those who keep the commandments of God and hold the testimony of Jesus.[3]

This vivid apocalyptic imagery has come to be understood as Mary, Queen of Heaven. Although the story of the birth in Revelation does not coincide with the gospels or with the life of Jesus on Earth, nevertheless the story is understood as the cosmic image of Mary. "A woman clothed with the sun, with the moon under her feet, and on her head a crown of twelve stars" has been reproduced in artistic depictions of Mary down through the ages. But the image of a woman clothed with the sun has also taken on a life of its own in certain parts of the church. Perhaps the most dynamic understanding of Mary is currently within the Mexican-American Episcopal congregations and comes from devotion to Our Lady of Guadalupe.

The Virgin of Guadalupe appeared to an Aztec peasant who had been given the baptismal name of Juan Diego (who was canonized in the Roman Catholic Church in 2002) on a hill outside what is now Mexico City, in December 1531. The place was originally called Tepeyec. Gradually it became known as Guadalupe, but the reason for the name change is unclear. The apparition of Mary came at a time when the native dark-skinned people of Mexico were demoralized by the culture and religious traditions of the conquering Spanish. Mary appeared on a site that was sacred to one of the major Aztec goddesses, Tonantzin. She told the bewildered peasant to go and tell the bishop to build a church on the site. Juan Diego did as she asked, and was dismissed as a teller of tales. But the vision came again, a beautiful dark-skinned woman, and she told the peasant: "Am I not here, your mother? Are you not under my shadow and my protection?" Eventually the bishop asked Juan Diego to bring him a sign as proof of his vision.

The apparition provided a sign—an abundance of Castillian roses that normally do not grow in December in the desert around Mexico City. Juan Diego gathered them in his tilma, a woven overgarment somewhat like a serape. He rushed to show the roses to the bishop, and when he let them fall from his garment, there appeared on his garment the image of the woman who had spoken to him, painted, apparently, by the roses that he had carried. The bishop fell to his knees, and subsequently built the church she had requested on the site she indicated.[4]

Her image remains on Juan Diego's tilma, which has survived for over four and a half centuries, despite the fragile fabric it is painted on. The picture on the tilma is that of a brown-skinned, pregnant woman, surrounded by the rays of the sun and standing on the moon. She is very much like the image described in the Revelation to John. The tilma remains in the shrine on the site where the vision appeared and the first church was built. Because of the great popularity of the shrine, a new and larger basilica has been built. The place teems with life; approximately fifteen million visitors come each year. The huge new basilica is designed to offer a view of the tilma to all who worship there. A closer view is available by going on a walkway, which passes beneath the tilma both coming and going.

Pilgrims to Mexico City may be surprised to learn that the Anglican Church in Mexico does not share with their compatriots a devotion to the Virgin of Guadalupe. Carlos Touché Porter, bishop of the Anglican church of Mexico, explained that it is often difficult to extricate the Virgin of Guadalupe from the identity of the Mexican people. For example, the colors of the Mexican flag are taken from the picture on the tilma. But the Anglican Church in Mexico has a different view of Our Lady of Guadalupe, which is buttressed by three interwoven and complex strands.

First, there are questions about the miracle itself. Some church historians have pointed out significant questions about the events of December 1531, and noted the lack of any mention of Juan Diego and the appearance of the Virgin in church records until a century later. Though a shrine was dedicated to Our Lady of Guadalupe at the site, dating from around 1530, the primary concern of the church at that time appears to be that the native people were worshiping Tonantzin under the guise of Our Lady of Guadalupe. Some suggest that the name and image of Guadalupe are simply carried over from a similar image called the Virgin of Guadalupe, in the Estramadura region of Spain. The image is a dark fourteenth-century image, a "Black Madonna," from the province that was the home of many of the conquistadores, including Hernando Cortés.[5] In addition, some students of scripture have pointed out that the recorded words of the Virgin of Guadalupe are not consonant with those of Mary in the New Testament. For example, the Virgin of Guadalupe asked Juan Diego to "erect my temple on the plain,"[6] whereas Mary in scripture directed people toward Jesus, saying, "Do whatever he tells you."[7]

Second, Mexican Anglicans expressed concern about the pivotal place of Guadalupe. The great emphasis on the Virgin of Guadalupe in the Roman Catholic Church in Mexico, where she often has a central place at the altar, has led the Anglican Church in Mexico to focus more specifically on the person and life of Jesus. This difference is particularly apparent in the iconography of the two traditions. In the Anglican Church in Mexico, Mary is not depicted as the Virgin of Guadalupe but rather as another image, such as Our Lady of Walsingham, and she is not the central image of the altar.

Third, the two Christian traditions have an embattled history over Guadalupe. In 1878 twenty-two members of the fledgling Anglican Communion in the village of Atzala, State of Puebla, were slaughtered by religious zealots, crying: "Long live Guadalupe. Death to those who do not adore her." Those members of the congregation that survived were expelled from the village and not allowed to return. Pointedly and poignantly, the martyrdom of those Anglican Christians was done on December 12, the feast of Our Lady of Guadalupe.[8]

Lydia Lopez, a Mexican-American Episcopalian who serves as public affairs officer for the Diocese of Los Angeles, is aware of the history of the Anglican Church of Mexico and the questions surrounding Our Lady of Guadalupe. Yet despite the difficulties some have raised about Guadalupe, she says: "The story of Guadalupe appearing to the peasant, Diego, is a wonderful story. Whether it happened doesn't matter. Even if it was 'a PR thing,' it's marvelous, and if it really happened, all the better." For her, Guadalupe is a part of her Mexican heritage, and an important part. She hastens to add that being an Anglican in the United States is a different experience from being one in Mexico, where the dominant culture is Roman Catholic.

The Episcopal Church is growing in the Mexican-American community, and new members are not always aware of the Anglican history in Mexico. Our Lady of Guadalupe has come to be identified with the Mexican-American people; she is clearly and easily their patron saint. Her image emblazoned on a flag became an important symbol as Cesar Chávez and Delores Huerta led the farmworkers to seek better working and living conditions, and she remains a vibrant link between the spiritual and the political to this day. Her image pervades the culture and is spread through immigration.

Contemporary Mexican-American artists depict Our Lady of Guadalupe in startlingly fresh ways. Isabel Martinez shows her holding her green card; Ester Hernandez shows her giving a Kung Fu–type side kick; Isis Rodrigues shows her riding a motorcycle; Yolanda Lopez shows Saint Ann at the sewing machine making the veil covered with stars while the infant Virgin of Guadalupe plays on the floor below. José Antonio Burciaga, in a mural showing the last supper of Chicano heroes, portrays Our Lady of Guadalupe above them all.

The shrine of Our Lady of Guadalupe is just one example of numerous shrines to Mary, and Mexico is not unique in having a shrine to Mary on the site where an ancient goddess was worshiped. The cults of various goddesses, Near Eastern mother divinities, and Celtic and Germanic deities, which were associated with ancient mountain, water, and tree sanctuaries, were easily transformed to the cult of Mary. Just as we associate a mother with a specific location or house, so the cult of Mary seemed to continually find new local habitations. It was so much the case throughout Christian history that the proliferation of holy sites to Mary was among the concerns of the sixteenth-century reformers. It is well known that the church incorporated sites of earlier religions and replaced their images with Christian ones. And yet while the phenomenon may have begun with political overtones, the theological underpinnings were what enabled the shrines to flourish. A. N. Allchin writes: "She it is who, by her vocation to be the place of God, and by her fulfillment of that vocation, reveals the true destiny of all places, indeed of all humankind and all creation, which shares in that high calling to become the place of God's inhabitation. . . . The very nature of time and space is illumined and transformed when the divine presence is made known within it."[9]

MARY AND GOD THE MOTHER

The importance of Our Lady of Guadalupe and her centrality in Mexican culture push to the fore the often neglected motherhood of God. Though the Bible contains images of the female nature and motherhood of God, they have largely been obscured by the more prevalent male and paternal images. But images of God as female are clearly there. The prophet Hosea envisions God as an angry and protective mother bear;[10] God speaks to the prophet Isaiah, saying, "I will cry out like a woman in labor, I will gasp and pant."[11] In one of his parables, Jesus likens the searching love of God to a woman who has lost a coin.[12]

Our tradition of faith is not static, but dynamic and alive. As our understanding of God evolves, changes, and matures, edges of theology blur and images morph into other images. God is our mother as well as our father, and at times we long for the mothering of God. But how do we address and worship the mothering God? For those who long to experience the maternal aspect of God, one impediment is our traditional language of prayer. Centuries of praying to God as Father have extended roots deep into the collective culture as well as the individual psyche, where they powerfully resist change.

Contemporary Christians know intellectually that God encompasses both female and male, but they still struggle to find creative liturgical language that will celebrate that fact. Awkwardness seems to be part of the process. Liturgical prayer struggles to balance meaning with verbal music; poetry is at times sacrificed for justice. We see the difficulty in the mundane problem of how we address female priests: Although "Father Chris" rolls trippingly off the tongue, "Mother Chris" comes less easily. Once we have moved beyond the maleness or femaleness of God, we will discover that service, not gender, is the primary characteristic of God. But in the meantime, our patriarchal language makes it difficult to envision God the Mother, and so people often turn to Mary when they seek the feminine face of God.

The ease with which people have confused Mary with God the Mother may result from one of the early church's titles for Mary—Mother of God—which was given amid great controversy. It occurred at the Third Ecumenical Council, which took place in 431 at the site of the Church of Saint Mary, in Ephesus. Some of the church fathers, championed by Cyril of Alexandria, wanted to give Mary the title of *Theotokos,* "God-bearer" or "Mother of God," but others said that she was actually only the "Mother of Jesus." This gave rise to the question of whether Jesus was a human being closely united to God, a superior kind of prophet, or God in human guise. What the council stated was that he was a single, undivided person who was both God and human at once. Consequently, the church gave Mary the name *Theotokos,* or "Mother of God," which remains her title in Christianity today. The term *Theotokos* first came from the title given to Mary by her cousin Elizabeth, when Elizabeth referred to Mary as "the mother of my Lord." The fifth-century bishops at Ephesus, in affirming Mary's title as Mother of God, actually reaffirmed the ancient formulation of the faith of Israel, "Hear, O Israel: the Lord our God, the Lord is one," a statement reaffirmed by Jesus in the gospels.[13] It is important to recognize that the title Mother of God means not that Mary was the source of Jesus' divinity, but that she gave Jesus life.

Confusing Mary with God the Mother is not a new difficulty. In the fourth century, a group of women known as Collyridians worshiped Mary as Queen of Heaven, and invoking her name, made ritual offerings of bread. The cult flourished and spread widely. Epiphanius attacked it as a heresy, but it is one that predates any Christian reverence for Mary, and it may have been a precursor to the cult of Mary that developed in the Middle Ages.[14]

It is evident in the gospels that Mary did not view herself in a grand or cosmological way. In both of the infancy narratives that speak of the miraculous conception of Jesus, we are told that he was conceived by the Holy Spirit and that the mother was a young woman. However, the Gospel of John takes the origins of Jesus back well before his conception and birth, into preexistent time. John begins his gospel with these words: "In the beginning was the Word, and the Word was with God, and the Word was God. He was in the beginning with God. All things came into being through him."[15] John was neither aware of nor interested in the means of Christ's conception; for him Christ was essentially "I Am." Eventually Christian theology harmonized conception theology with preexistent theology in formulating the Doctrine of the Incarnation.[16]

Clearly, Mary was not preexistent in the gospels; she was a historical figure who bore Jesus into the world and knew herself to be a creature of the creator, albeit one with an unusual calling. Conflating turns of phrase in these matters can give rise to a host of problems. Though Mary is understood as the Mother of God, that does not imply equivalence with the Fatherhood of God as Jesus understood it. The clear need for balance in the traditional patriarchal language of the Trinity is not solved by stretching the role of Mary beyond her scope as first in the communion of saints.

One of the major theologians of the Anglican tradition, Julian of Norwich, addressed the issue of gender and God over five hundred years ago. She lived a cloistered life in the bustling fourteenth-century city of Norwich, northeast of London, and gave spiritual counsel from her cell. In addition, she has the distinction of being the first woman to write a book in English. She was a visionary, and perceived the mothering nature of God, but she did so in an unusual way. She did not perceive the Creator God as God the Mother; rather, she perceived Jesus, who clearly came to Earth as a man, as a mother. She saw in him the nurturing and compassion that are the essence of motherhood. Mary factors into that equation through the influence of her parenting. Julian wrote, "So our Lady is our mother, in whom we are all enclosed and born of her in Christ, for she who is mother of our savior is mother of all who are saved in our savior; and our savior is our true Mother, in whom we are endlessly born and out of whom we shall never come."[17] Julian's understanding of the gender issues of God gives us some new perspectives, but it still leaves a desire in many for the feminine body to be valued, understood, and literally incorporated into the Godhead. And so, once again, believers turn to Mary.

Elizabeth A. Johnson writes of Mary: "For innumerable believers, this village woman, mother of Jesus, honored as Mother of God, functions as an icon of the maternal God, revealing the divine love as merciful, close, interested in the poor and weak, ready to hear human needs, related to the earth, trustworthy, and profoundly attractive. In devotion to her as a compassionate mother who will not let one of her children be lost, what is actually being mediated is a most appealing experience of God."[18]

The sheltering, embracing, cosmic image frequently given to Mary is actually better understood as God the Holy Spirit, the aspect of God in which we live and move and have our being. The Third Person of the Trinity, the Holy Spirit, the Comforter, the Advocate, is increasingly designated as feminine because the Hebrew word *ruah*, meaning "Spirit of God," is grammatically feminine; and the Greek word *pneuma*, meaning "wind" or "breath," is grammatically neuter. Although the Latin word *spiritus* is grammatically masculine, it is not incorrect to refer to the Holy Spirit as "She." A contemporary hymn celebrates the Holy Spirit as "sailing on the wind, her wings flashing in the sun . . . full of laughter, full of light, she flies on."[19] In the Nicene Creed, the Holy Spirit is acknowledged as the aspect of God that gives life, through whom Jesus was conceived, as well as the voice that speaks through prophecy.[20] The Holy Spirit was clearly active in the life of Mary, both as the spirit behind the voice of prophecy and as the spirit through which Jesus was conceived. Yet because the Holy Spirit is the aspect of God that is most mysterious—God among us, God between us, and God inside us—many Christians do not fully appreciate that dimension of the Trinity.

INTERCESSOR

Another means of involving Mary in the lives of the faithful, but one that does not confuse her with God, is to view her as an intercessor. Of all the saints, she is the one most often asked to intercede for us. And yet that is problematic for many; for example, one Methodist student who objected to invoking the name of the Virgin Mary, and to whom Archbishop Desmond Tutu responded with a laugh and these words "You've done away with the whole theory of intercession."[21] The *Book of Common Prayer* defines *intercession* as prayer that "brings before God the needs of others," and it defines the *communion of saints* as those "bound together in Christ by sacrament, prayer, and praise."[22] Although many do not invoke the saints, for others, trusting in the prayers of the saints means it is not far fetched to ask the saints to pray for them. However, it is one thing to ask a saint to pray for us, and a very different thing to pray to that same being. C. S. Lewis wrote: "While Christendom is divided about the rationality and even the lawfulness of praying to the saints, we are all agreed about praying with them. 'With angels and archangels and all the company of heaven.'"[23]

In one instance in the gospels, Mary interceded to Jesus on behalf of others. It was at the wedding in Cana. All she said to Jesus was "They have no wine."[24] Those four words summarized her concern for the bride and groom, the families of the couple, and the community. She saw the need and asked Jesus to help. And although she was initially rebuffed, he did do as she asked. A great many of the prayers of the faithful are intercessory prayers, and come when people perceive the needs of others and ask for God's help. The gospels note other instances of people asking for Jesus' help on behalf of others, but the story of the wedding at Cana is designated as the first miracle, and consequently set a precedent of intercession that other people followed. Mary and intercessory prayer have been linked down the ages. Intercession is the turning of concern for others into compassionate and creative activity. It could also be called godly gossip. When we ask God's help for others, we set in motion forces that can do more than we can imagine. In addition, asking for God's help can lead the one who prays to productive and helpful aid, ranging from solicitous conversation and casseroles to struggling for peace and justice. Intercession nurtures the community aspect of the church by fostering compassion and generating creative congregational responses.

The roots of Mary's particular role as intercessor possibly come from third-century apocryphal writings concerning the death of Mary. Those stories, called Transitus Mariae, contain this prayer of Mary to Christ, "Give your aid to every one calling upon, or praying to, or naming the name of your handmaid." Jesus responded, saying, "Every soul that calls upon your name shall not be ashamed, but will find mercy and support and confidence both in the world that now is and that which is to come in the presence of God in heaven."[25] These writings, like the Proevangelium of James, are not considered part of the scriptural canon, yet they pointedly and appealingly tell of Mary's willingness to intercede.

But do Anglican churches encourage their members to ask for Mary's aid? Officially in Anglicanism there is no direct invocation of Mary. She is viewed solely in relation to the Christ event. She is understood as the gate of the Incarnation, and one who in her life functioned as an example of faith and a model of virtue, as is apparent in an early nineteenth-century hymn by Bishop Reginald Heber. The hymn clearly points to Jesus, but the words honor Mary.

> Virgin born, we bow before thee: blessed was the womb that bore thee;—
> Mary, Mother meek and mild,—blessed was she in her Child.
>
> Blessed was the breast that fed thee; blessed was the hand that led thee;
> blessed was the parent's eye that watched thy slumbering infancy.
>
> Blessed she by all creation, who brought forth the world's salvation,
> and blessed they, forever blest, who love thee most and serve thee best.[26]

Mary is not addressed. She is honored through Jesus. She shows us how to receive the Word and the sacraments. She is first among the saints, but she has no standing by herself; her merit is entirely bound with Jesus, and her role in this hymn is seen as historical rather than contemporary. However, another hymn, written only two generations later, addresses the entire church in heaven and specifically addresses Mary with the words "Thou bearer of the eternal Word, most gracious, magnify the Lord."[27]

Though it may appear that a shift in thought has occurred, what we see in the second hymn is the resurgence of an old tradition of direct address to Mary, which had a long history in England. The earliest surviving prayer to Mary is from the fourth century, and possibly older (this Greek papyrus is now in the John Rylands Library in Manchester, England), and the earliest prayer written in England is an Anglo-Latin poem by Aldhelm in 685. In it Aldhelm beseeches Mary to listen to the people, "who moisten their withered faces with streams of tears and, on bended leg, strike the earth with their knees."[28] Uniquely among the saints, Mary was viewed as both powerful and particularly receptive to human misery and need. An especially beautiful prayer to her was written by the Venerable Bede, the great eighth-century historian of England:

Sublime among the glittering stars of the apostles,
and filled with the fire of the Holy Spirit,
thou singest concordant praise.
O mother of Christ,
may thine intercession commend to God
the praise which we supplicants
bring him in our hymns.[29]

That the faithful of medieval England put their faith in Mary's intercession was clearly shown by the popular "Miracles of the Virgin," a genre of folktales. These flourished from the end of the thirteenth century until the close of the Middle Ages. One that is still read and enjoyed today is Geoffrey Chaucer's "Prioress's Tale."[30] Medieval artists depicted people of all walks of life sheltering beneath Mary's outstretched mantle or cape, to show that all of humanity was under her protection. But change came with the English Reformation. Thomas Cranmer effectively removed intercession to Mary from the 1552 *Book of Common Prayer* onward, and the removal impacted private devotions, although it did not completely change them.[31] Some in the Anglican Communion continued and still continue, unofficially, to ask Mary to intercede for them. A seventeenth-century Anglican bishop clarified the differences that the Reformation caused by pointing out a significant change in terminology: "The mere addressing of angels and saints, inviting them to pray with us and for us to God, in the same way that we ask good people during their lifetime here to intercede with God for us, . . . we with those Protestants who prefer to speak more clearly and carefully in this matter, call advocation, rather than invocation, a calling unto rather than a calling upon."[32] While invocation means calling upon higher power, advocation means calling for the prayerful assistance of others. An Anglican understanding of intercession means we are asking others to pray to God on our behalf, and we recognize that God alone has the power to answer or respond to those prayers.

Though such prayer is not officially part of Anglican piety, it has been a part of our Anglican history, and remains a practice for a small but significant number within our tradition. Those who do not ask for Mary's intercession may wonder why others do. Perhaps it is because they view Mary as their spiritual mother, or perhaps it is because she, of all the saints, came closest to touching redemption in the person of her son. There is also merit in the observation that as an intercessor, Mary fulfills what has been the natural role of mothers in our patriarchal culture: the "power behind the throne."[33] Where the judgment of God is emphasized, she has been viewed as the softer route to the Almighty; the tenderhearted mother who has God's ear. Although contemporary Anglican theology follows the thinking of Julian of Norwich, who wrote that there is no wrath in God as we have come to understand God in Christ, nevertheless a tenderhearted advocate may be helpful en route to that understanding. As a contemporary spiritual director says, "The prayers of Mary and the saints are joined to God's own compassionate love in quenching the wrath within ourselves."[34]

THE ROSARY AND THE ANGELUS

Several years ago I went on pilgrimage to the shrine of Dame Julian of Norwich, and later was fortunate to meet with Robert Llewellyn, an Anglican priest, noted spiritual director, and former Chaplain to the Shrine. I happened to arrive on his birthday, and although he was in his nineties, he regaled me with cake and tea. A strong advocate of the Rosary, he asked me if I knew it. I confessed I was just learning it, and he offered to teach me. For instruction he used a large wooden rosary with beads the size of marbles, and had me say the first sentence of each bead prayer while he said the second. He was eager for my theological comfort, and offered a number of Christ-centered prayers as well as the traditional Hail Mary. In the responsive sharing of the prayer, I gained an appreciation of the rosary not only as a prayer tool but also as a means of communal meditation and prayer.

The Rosary and the Angelus are the best known Marian prayers. The rosary began as a prayer tool that originally came from the East (possibly originating from "worry beads," strings of beads initially used to relieve anxiety, then gradually moving to religious practice), from Hinduism through Buddhism and Islam, and finally spreading to Christianity. In the ninth century, Celtic monks used a string of beads to help them keep count for the singing of the psalms. The word *bede* is actually an Anglo-Saxon word for "prayer."[35] From it grew a simpler version for use by the illiterate laity, who were encouraged to count beads to assist them as they said the Lord's Prayer 150 times (the number of the psalms). As a result, the first name given the Rosary in the British Isles was Paternoster. William of Malmesbury, in his history of England, tells that Lady Godiva of Coventry, in 1041 left in her will a circlet of gems on which she used to say her prayers. She specified that it was to be hung around a statue of the virgin after her death. It is one of the earliest accounts of the rosary in England.[36] and reminds us that rosary beads can be beautiful and a pleasure for the eye as well as the hand.

Usually fifty beads were used, and the user could go around the beads three times. In a parallel growth, some of the faithful who were particular advocates of Mary began to repeat the words of the Hail Mary for each bead. Those words come directly from scripture, and combine the greeting of the angel Gabriel to Mary[37] and Elizabeth's greeting to her.[38] The combined words appeared for the first time in the sixth century in Antioch, and the name *Jesus* was added to emphasize the Christocentric nature of the prayer. The second sentence of the prayer, "Holy Mary, Mother of God, pray for us sinners now and at the hour of our death," uses the fourth-century title of *Theotokos,* and bases the rest of the phrase on the extrapolation that because Mary was deemed "full of grace," the faithful could directly ask for her intercession.

From these beginnings evolved a division of the beads into decades, or groups of ten, which were separated by additional beads. The beads were joined by a medallion, from which hung a short string of five beads ending with a cross or crucifix. To recite the traditional Rosary is to begin with the cross or crucifix, and holding it, recite the Apostles' Creed. Then moving up the short string of beads: at the first bead, say the Lord's Prayer; then at the next begins the Hail Mary, which is said for each of the next three beads, with the intention of increasing faith, hope, and charity. The words of the Hail Mary are as follows: "Hail Mary, full of grace, the Lord is with you; blessed are you among women and blessed is the fruit of your womb, Jesus. Holy Mary, Mother of God, pray for us sinners now and at the hour of our death. Amen."

The Gloria Patri is recited on the next bead. Then on the same bead, the Rosary begins with the Lord's Prayer. As our fingers move past the medallion, the Hail Mary is said on each of the beads for the decades of the circlet. At the end of each decade, on the intervening bead, a Gloria Patri is recited to end the decade, and the Lord's Prayer is said on the same bead to begin the next decade. At the end of the circlet, a prayer such as Hail Holy Queen or the Collect for the Annunciation is recited while holding the medallion.

Gradually the decades came to be associated with meditations on the life of Mary, and they were separated into the five Joyful Mysteries, the five Sorrowful Mysteries, and the five Glorious Mysteries. Most of the mysteries of the Rosary are based on scriptural events. The Joyful Mysteries include the Annunciation, the Visitation, the Nativity, the Presentation in the Temple, and Finding Jesus in the Temple, and they can be doorways into meditation and deeper understanding of scripture. The Sorrowful Mysteries include the Agony in Gethsemane, the Scourging, the Crown of Thorns, the Carrying of the Cross, and the Crucifixion, and they offer a clear counterpoint to the first five mysteries. A book on the rosary, titled *Five for Sorrow, Ten for Joy*,[39] reminds us that the traditional rosary is weighted on the side of joy. The traditional Glorious Mysteries are the Resurrection, the Ascension, and the Descent of the Holy Spirit, but the last two of the Glorious Mysteries are not scripturally based. The penultimate is Mary's Assumption into heaven, and the last is the Coronation of Mary. A revised set of Glorious Mysteries using only gospel material could be the Transfiguration, the Last Supper, the Resurrection, the Ascension, and the Coming of the Holy Spirit.[40]

While the Rosary is certainly identified as a Marian prayer, it need not be restricted to that. It is simply a tool, and a variety of forms of the tool exist. Orthodox Christians use the rosary to repeat the Jesus Prayer, "Lord Jesus Christ, have mercy on me." Anglican schemes of praying the rosary, which focus on healing, the sacraments, thanksgiving, or the Resurrection have also been devised. There are many options in using the rosary. Recent years have also seen the evolution of a different configuration of the rosary itself, which is called an Anglican rosary. Instead of five Decades, it has four Weeks, and instead of ten beads to a Decade, there are seven beads to a Week. In breaking out of the traditional form, additional freedom and energy have emerged: One particularly appealing version repeats the words of Julian of Norwich, "All shall be well, all shall be well, and all manner of things shall be well." Those who use the Anglican rosary are encouraged to experiment and find the prayers that work best for them. One colleague wears her rosary as a necklace, and enjoys praying with it throughout the day. While her prayer use of the rosary does not include prayers involving Mary, she feels that the tactile nature of the rosary will help bring Anglicans back into awareness of the physicality of prayer, which eventually will lead to Mary.[41] Recently, beaded prayer bracelets have emerged, which offer additional opportunities for innovative daily prayers.

The Angelus, another well-known Marian prayer, probably originated in the eleventh century, and the prayer scheme was designated to be said with the tolling of the curfew bell in the evening. The Angelus bell is rung three times in groups of three strokes, with pauses between them, and then nine strokes altogether. Each group of three strokes has a scripturally based versicle, and the first group commemorates the angelic salutation:

V. The angel of the Lord announced unto Mary,
R. And she conceived by the Holy Spirit.

The traditional Hail Mary follows each versicle and response. The second group of bell strokes commemorates Mary's words to the angel:

V. Behold the handmaid of the Lord.
R. Be it unto me according to thy Word.

Following a second recitation of the Hail Mary, the third group of three bell strokes commemorates the Incarnation:[42]

V. And the word was made flesh,
R. And dwelt among us.

After the third Hail Mary, there is a concluding versicle and response:

V. Pray for us, O holy Mother of God.
R. That we may be made worthy of the promises of Christ.[43]

The prayer concludes with the Collect for the Annunciation or a collect for the Incarnation. This brief prayer scheme with its threefold Hail Mary was said three times daily: at six in the morning, at noon, and at the curfew bell in the evening. The Angelus was based on the routine ringing of church bells, and because church bells ringing the hours are no longer part of most of our daily lives, the Angelus has been prayed only when an effort is made by churches to perpetuate the tradition.

The Angelus and the Rosary differ in that the Angelus is a communal call to prayerful attention in the midst of the day, and the Rosary is a meditative and contemplative scheme for use at any time. Though both enable us to focus on God, the repetitive nature of the Rosary offers a practical means of quieting the mind. Increasing numbers of Anglicans are learning the Rosary, both in the traditional Marian form and in the many varieties of the Anglican form. They are incorporating this prayer tool into their prayer life, as Christians have done for centuries.

The use of the rosary illustrates a gradual softening between what was once a high-Church and a low-Church approach to Mary. A tool that was once identified solely with intercessory prayer to Mary has broadened out to a variety of uses, some of which lead back to a new understanding and appreciation of her. Another example is the growing appreciation of the importance of Our Lady of Guadalupe in the Mexican-American community, and her inclusion in Episcopal churches across the country. Furthermore, the Episcopal Church continues in efforts toward inclusive liturgical language, and we now are much more aware of the need to acknowledge and celebrate the feminine dimension of God as well as women's roles in the story of salvation. We now turn to explore Mary in the church and the culture: how she has served as a guide in daily living and as a window into spiritual growth.

QUESTIONS FOR STUDY, PRAYER, AND REFLECTION

1. Have you ever asked Mary to pray for you? Why or why not? Do you pray for others? Have you ever experienced godly gossip? ungodly gossip?

2. Do you understand and experience God as a loving parent? If God is a father to you, can you also experience God as a mother? If Jesus, as Dame Julian suggests, is God our Mother, how do we incorporate the feminine body and female experience into our faith?

3. The woman in the twelfth chapter of Revelation is seen as both vulnerable and powerful. Does she enrich your understanding of Mary? How?

4. The heritage of Mexican Anglicans and that of Mexican-Americans coming to the Episcopal Church in the United States offer two very different experiences of the Virgin of Guadalupe. How might both experiences be honored?

5. Have you ever used a prayer tool such as the rosary or a labyrinth? Have you found such tools helpful? How does using them differ from your other experiences of prayer? Have they been aids to intercessory prayer?

7 🕮 As Paradigm

"Here is your mother." (John 19:27)

THE BLESSED MOTHER

I wonder how she felt when
men leered at her swollen belly,
when women joked and winked as
she walked slowly by. But she kept on
eating the bread of sincerity and
tasting the wine of amazement.

And when murder reigned and
she could protect him, when rocks
loomed jagged and menacing,
she took him and fled to Egypt.

How was it then, when he had grown,
to have village voices say her child
was mad, possessed by scores of devils?
And, as if that were not enough,
how had she burned at his rebuffs,
and how long before she could receive
his challenges as larger wisdom?

And when murder reigned again and
she could not protect him, when rocks
loomed jagged and menacing, and tombs

opened their mouths, she stood,
her arms empty, and howled at the sky.

It is a long journey through this life.
There are enough wounds to teach us rage
or lead us into ruin. But she kept on
and learned to love, following the child who
taught her, a part of her becoming
translucent, a great soul that magnified
the greater comprehending soul
of everything that lives.

Mary's Domain

Several years ago the Associated Press ran a photograph from Saint Michael's Church in Wheeling, West Virginia. It showed a statue of Mary with a nest of young robins in her crown. Three baby birds were in the nest, and all of them had their beaks open singing for food. It was a rich image showing new life and new song in the springtime of the year, when we celebrate the Annunciation. March 25, nine months before Christmas, is when we remember that Mary conceived the new life of Christ, and she, like the young robins, celebrated that spring with her own magnificent song.

Mary is and has been many things throughout the ages. She is a biblical personage, first among the communion of saints, and a paradigm of how we see ourselves and live our lives. As a paradigm and an exemplar of holiness, she is a source of self-understanding for those who seek to follow Christ, and her own path inspires and parallels many of our own. Her story calls into question the consensus of secular culture and challenges the status quo. The word *paradigm* means "an example or pattern," but it also has a grammatical usage, and means the full conjugation of a verb. It is interesting to think of Mary as a paradigm in that context, because she carried the Word of God and went on to experience that Word, which was and is, first and foremost, a verb, in its many conjugations.

Mary's life has been a source of reflection for people throughout the centuries. The faithful have seen their own lives mirrored in her joys and sorrows and found the study of her life to be a help and a consolation. While we recognize Mary's influence in much of Western Europe, we may not realize that England was particularly devoted to Mary, and known as Mary's "dower," or "dowry." This referred to the wealth or estate that was given on behalf of a bride, and England acquired this title because of the great number of churches and cathedrals dedicated to Mary. Traces of the former pervasiveness of the glory of "Mary's dower" can now be found only in chapel and church names, and in the names of a few English wild-flowers such as marigold and lady's slipper. But at one time, almost every wild and domestic flower had a name connected with Mary. For example, primrose was known as Our Lady's candlestick; morning glory was the Virgin's mantle; foxglove was Lady's thimble; daffodil was Mary's star; the tiny blue flowers of forget-me-not were eyes of Mary; and lily of the valley was Our Lady's tears.[1]

It is important to note that Mary was revered more in England than she was in Italy, Spain, or France. She was the focus of paintings and statuary, and her joys and sorrows were detailed in stained glass. She was also celebrated in poetry and folktales; and the oral tradition of storytelling, alongside the ancient tradition of stories of Mary's early life, meant that many extrabiblical stories about Mary were shared and embroidered. For instance, the second-century apocryphal Book of James became the basis of a famous cycle of medieval mystery plays. It told of Mary's unique childhood, her betrothal to Joseph, the Annunciation, and the Nativity.[2] In addition, festivals throughout the year celebrated her. It was English theologians such as Anselm of Canterbury who wrote hymns to her purity, and the Cistercian abbot Aelred of Rievaulx who made dramatic efforts to elevate her above other disciples and promoted a feast for her Immaculate Conception. English people of that time loved to celebrate her, argue over her, and enlist her as an intercessor on their behalf. The Wilton Diptych of the late fourteenth century shows Richard II kneeling before her as she stands regally arrayed and surrounded by hosts of angels. For centuries she was both Queen of Heaven and Queen of England.

As mentioned earlier, many ways in which devotion to Mary was expressed changed dramatically with the English Reformation of 1529. Much of the religious literature and devotional art was lost when Henry VIII destroyed the monasteries (and a great deal more was lost when Oliver Cromwell and the Roundheads defaced church images in the seventeenth century). The reformed church abandoned much of medieval piety and custom, a large share of which involved Mary. But devotion to Mary was not completely eradicated by the English Reformation; a good share of it was transferred to the new political cult of the Virgin Queen of the Renaissance, Elizabeth I. When Elizabeth shrewdly took the title Virgin Queen, she garnered a portion of the spiritual as well as political devotion that had once been directed to the Virgin Queen of Heaven. She was aware that many of the powerful medieval guilds, colleges, fraternal groups, and religious houses had Mary as their patron. Elizabeth's able leadership, combined with England's traditional affection for the Virgin Mary, intensified the power and reputation of the great sixteenth-century monarch.

Another large portion of the zeal Mary once inspired in England found expression in the enhancement of the Doctrine of the Incarnation, the doctrine that God took on human flesh and lived among us, which eventually became distinguished as the doctrine most emphasized in the Anglican tradition. Images of the Madonna and Child speak for the Incarnation, of Christ being born among us, as no other image can. The Doctrine of the Incarnation enshrines Mary's importance in the story of salvation, and through it English theologians continued to honor her. The seventeenth-century Anglican preacher Mark Frank explained that because Jesus is our Lord, it follows that Mary must be our Lady. He says that all her worthiness and honor come from Christ, and yet he goes on to say, "Christ in her be the business: that we take pattern from the angel, to give her no more than is due to her, yet to be sure to give her that."

Mary came to be known as Our Lady, and the Feast of the Annunciation known as Lady Day. Lady Chapels and votive shrines to Mary in smaller churches continue to be part of the Anglican and Episcopal traditions, and they continue to be places where believers ask for intercessory assistance from her. While some contemporary Christians are, understandably, uncomfortable with terms such as Lord and Lady, which have roots in political aristocracy, others find that their theological use reworks the meaning to give them a different significance.

A Home in England

As Mary's example brings honor to the life of wife and mother, her house in Nazareth, or a replica of it, would have a special attraction. Such has been the case in England since the eleventh century. Around 1061 Dame Richeldis Faverches, lady of the manor of Walsingham Parva, had a vision while her husband was away on a crusade to the Holy Land in which she was taken three times to the house of the Annunciation in Nazareth, and Mary told her to note its dimensions and make an exact replica in Walsingham, a tiny village in East Anglia. Thus began what came to be known as England's Nazareth, the most popular Marian shrine in the British Isles. The Pymson Ballad, published circa 1496, tells the story of the shrine:

Of this chapell se here the fundacyon,
Bylded the yere of Crystes incarnacyon,
A thousande complete syxty and one,
The tyme of sent Edward kyng of this region.[3]

The exact site where the house was to be built was revealed by the failure of morning dew to cover the spot. Two dry spots were found, and when the carpenters tried to erect the house on the first site, the ballad says, "no pece with oder woulde agre with geometrye."[4] Legend says that the following night Mary herself moved the house to the second site. A wooden statue of the Madonna and Child at the site was soon credited with miraculous healings, and water with reputed healing properties from two wells drew many with infirmities. An Augustinian priory was attached to the shrine in the middle of the twelfth century. Soon there grew a pilgrimage site to rival Santiago de Compostela, and even Rome. Kings and queens came barefoot to pay homage, some of them seeking miraculous aid in conceiving an heir.

But even Walsingham did not escape the Reformation. Henry VIII, the last royal pilgrim, destroyed the attached priory and had the statue of the virgin publicly burned at Chelsea in 1539. Although Henry VIII dissolved the shrine, it is worth noting that in his will, he bequeathed his soul to Our Lady of Walsingham. The Anglican shrine was revived in 1921, and there are now Anglican, Roman Catholic, and Orthodox chapels in the small village in northwest Norfolk.

To this day the village remains peaceful and untouched by much of modern life. Though the Anglican shrine is an active pilgrimage site, it retains a quiet, homelike atmosphere with inviting worship spaces, peaceful gardens, and comfortable amenities. The statue of Our Lady of Walsingham, which is modeled on the original that was destroyed, is a compelling image of a powerful, enthroned Madonna, similar to the strong, seated figures of the "Black Madonnas" that have drawn pilgrims all over the world. The shrine itself, steeped in centuries of prayer, gives the pilgrim an occasion to reflect on the home in which Jesus grew up.

Much of pre-Reformation piety involved taking the Holy Family as one's own. Because the shrine at Walsingham replicated the holy house in the English countryside, the English people of the Middle Ages found Mary accessible, local, and particularized. Likewise, liturgical art of Norfolk, the textile capital of England, often portrayed Mary sewing, and this made her seem even more like a local woman. The imagination of the pious followed suit: Margery Kempe, who was born in the late fourteenth century (and was the first person to write an autobiography in English), envisioned herself as midwife at the birth of Jesus. Later she meditated on the Crucifixion, and in her imagination went with the grieving Mary back to her house, where Margery prepared gruel for her. But Mary would not eat, and said to Margery, "Ah, daughter, I tell you truly there was never a woman on earth, who has such great cause to sorrow as I have, for there was never a woman in this world who bore a better child, nor a meeker child to his mother, than my child was to me."[5]

Although much of medieval piety may seem quaint, an awareness of Mary's accessibility made her a focus for piety. She was the perfect friend, neighbor, and parent. It is not surprising that a good deal of the medieval emphasis on Mary was related to childbearing, which, prior to modern medicine, was a prodigious physical risk for women. Women were given no relief for the physical pain of childbirth because pain was seen to be part of fallen creation and Eve's legacy. With no birth control, women generally had a child a year, and if they did not survive the ordeal long enough for the ritual cleansing, the "churching" of women, they could not be buried in sacred ground. Consequently, there was wide use of holy relics and images in conception and delivery. The most famous was the chemise of Mary, a length of white linen, which is the holy relic of Chartres Cathedral, in France. It is alleged to be a portion of the gown that Mary wore at the time of the Annunciation (some writings claim it was worn at the birth of Jesus), and is dated to be of the first century. Believed to have great healing powers, it was often taken to assist royalty in their childbearing. Pilgrims streamed to Chartres to avail themselves of its efficacy. Closeness to Mary's alleged belongings, places, and things has been an avenue of connection with the Holy Family for many of the faithful. Though Walsingham claimed a replica of the Holy House, in 1296, Loreto, Italy, claimed that the actual Holy House had been mysteriously flown there.

In addition to these European shrines, and subsequent ones over the centuries, a number of Marian sites in the Holy Land are still important destinations for pilgrims. For many, the opportunity to walk the countryside where Mary walked, breathe in the same air, smell bread cooking, and hear birds cry overhead offers an understanding of her life that reading and meditation cannot provide. The Holy Land is rich in such sites. In Bethlehem is the Nativity Church and the Milk Grotto, where Mary is reputed to have nursed the Christ child. In Nazareth is Mary's Well, the Church of Gabriel, the Church of Joseph, the Basilica of the Annunciation, and the home of the Holy Family. In Jerusalem is the home of Mary, Mary's Baths, the Holy Sepulchre (with a small monument showing where she was given into the care of John), the Arches of the Virgin (where legend says she met the risen Lord), and the Tomb of Mary. And in Egypt is an entire pilgrimage route, with sites marking the Holy Family's flight into Egypt.

Mary's Last House

Different sites appeal to pilgrims at different ages and stages of their own lives. A good friend of mine lost her son, an only child, when he was eighteen and they were living in the Middle East, living frugally in order to travel around the world when her husband's employment in the Middle East ended. After the shock of the unexpected death and funeral, they decided to continue with their travel plans. She was not active in a faith tradition, but was surprised when she went to a small stone house outside the ancient ruins of Ephesus, in Turkey. There, at a house called Meryam Ana, she said she felt the first peace she had felt in months. It is a house reputed to have been the last home of Mary, where the beloved disciple had taken her after Jesus, at the cross, had indicated that they were to care for each other as mother and son. My friend said she felt peace there, as if someone finally understood her experience, as if the free-floating pain had suddenly been anchored or lifted, found location and peace.

The house of Mary is a small stone building on the top of a high hill. A narrow road winds up from the plain below. It is a place where many pilgrims still go to touch Mary's life on this earth. It is a cool place, with the shade of oak and olive trees and the peaceful sound of running water pumped from a well. From there one can look down toward the ruins of what was once the thriving city of Ephesus, and beyond that toward the island of Patmos. It is a place conducive to solitude and thought, and one can imagine Mary spending her last years there in reflection and peace.

The ruins of the house were first seen in the vision of an eighteenth-century German nun, Sr. Anna Katherina Emmerich. She gave a precise description of the house, and in 1891 excavators discovered foundations that matched her description of the proportions. While claims for the validity of the vision can be questioned, the house has great popular appeal and draws pilgrims from all over the world. Mary was beloved by Christians in ancient Ephesus. Once the great seat of worship to Artemis, or Diana, Ephesus became a Christian community devoted to Mary, perhaps in part because she easily replaced worship of the powerful virgin goddess. Or it may have been that she did indeed spend her last years in those environs and was, for the Ephesians, a local saint.

Mary's bitter experience beholding her son's agony and death has made her a sympathetic figure to those whose lives are marked by similar suffering. Mothers down the ages have had not only to suffer but also to make choices, choices to trust in God and sometimes to trust in a future they would not see. Though Mary's experience is shared by sorrowing people all over the world and throughout all ages, her story speaks especially to women. Women constitute half of the world's population, yet they are disproportionately impoverished, uneducated, and unemployed.

SHARING SORROW

One such example of sorrowing and struggling women are the thousands of Latin American mothers who, in recent years, have had children and other family members abducted and designated "disappeared" by death squads. Many of these young people were tortured, murdered, and buried in mass graves. Others were drugged and dropped while asleep into the middle of the ocean to drown. Although these women begged for help from their governments, they were met with silence.

In 1976 a number of Argentinian mothers began a silent protest every week in front of government offices. Carrying photographs of their missing loved ones and wearing black dresses with white kerchiefs, these "mothers of the disappeared" marched around the plaza in witness. They also wore roses: a white rose if they hoped their loved one was still living and a red one for those whose loved one was known to be dead. From Argentina the march of the mothers spread to El Salvador and other countries. Some have had a sense that Mary, Madre Dolorosa, the sorrowing mother, walks with them and with all those who grieve and suffer from injustice, for they know that Mary's son was also abducted by a death squad, tortured, and killed, and so they trust that she understands their plight.

Another example of women who have found strength in Mary's example is Women in Black, a women's grassroots peace movement that began in the Holy Land in 1988. "Women in black" began with Palestinian and Israeli women wearing black as a sign of mourning, and standing together on Fridays to protest Israel's occupation of the West Bank and Gaza and to demand peace. Now it is an international network of women whose focus on peace in Mary's homeland has spread to protest war, hatred, and violence all over the world. Women stand in silent protest wearing black for bereavement. Their silence draws attention to the historic voicelessness of women.

In situations of injustice and suffering, Mary's words in the Magnificat have helped people see their own truth more clearly. In *Theology in a New Key: Responding to Liberation Theology,* Robert McAfee Brown recounts a Central American informal liturgy that involved reflecting on the Magnificat. One of those present had brought in a traditional painting of Mary as Queen of Heaven. After reading Mary's words in the Gospel of Luke, the priest asked the congregation what they thought of the image. The people said: "The Mary of the song would not be standing on the moon. She would be standing in the dirt and dust where we stand." The priest asked them to say more, and they went on: "The Mary of the song would not be wearing a crown. She would have on an old hat like the rest of us, to keep the sun from causing her to faint. The Mary of the song would not be wearing jeweled rings on her fingers. She would have rough hands like us. The Mary of the song would not be wearing a silk robe embroidered with gold. She would be wearing old clothes like the rest of us." Finally the people realized with some embarrassment: "It may be awful to say this, but it sounds as though Mary would look just like me! My feet are dirty, my hat is old, my hands are rough, and my clothes are torn."[6] From such recognition the people took on hope and began to see their lives with a new sense of purpose and empowerment.

Although centuries of honor have often rendered Mary as crowned and bejeweled, her identification with the poor still shines forth in the Magnificat. As Amma Syncletia wrote in the fourth century, "It is impossible for us to be surrounded by worldly honor and at the same time to bear heavenly fruit."[7] Mary was a model of one who spoke the truth to power, and her words and example have encouraged others, from African-American slaves to Central American peasants, to lift themselves, trusting in God's support. A prayer by Stuart Thomas for the Feast of the Annunciation echoes the words of the Magnificat for our time:

Lord God,
Through ocean's surge and spider's web,
By crushing of armies and cradling of children,
Your power is known in strength and gentleness.
We ask for your power in the world today
To pull down the mighty who abuse their privilege,
And help the frail and powerless lose their fear.

Lord God,
You planned the secrets of the earth
And know the bounds of human knowledge.

We ask for your wisdom in the world today
To enable the knowledge and technology of the few
    to be put at the disposal of all your children:
To ensure that earth's rulers and planners
    perceive the gifts and plight of the poor.

Lord God,
In the dawn of creation
And in the presence of your Son,
Your light shattered the force and lure of darkness.
We ask your help today
For those who, in public or personal life,
Are in the grip of that which is wicked:
For those who deal in rumors and perpetuate cheap gossip,
For those who are slaves to a vice they fear to name,
For those who have traded openness for secrecy,
    morality for money,
    love for lust.
We ask for a light, not to blind them
But to show them the way out of their darkness.

Lord God,
Through the cooperation of a woman
You gave us your Son, Jesus the Christ.
We ask your guidance in building right relationships
That start in each family and reach out to the people next door;
That start in our own community and reach over the barriers of
custom and prejudice to the community on the other side of town,
That start in our own country and reach beyond patriotism and
national pride to the nations of the world,
That start with our own color, and rejoice to claim as sisters and
brothers, women and men of every race.

Lord God,
Teach us today to rely on your strength,
    learn from your wisdom
    walk in your light and
    enjoy the company of your Spirit.
Thus, though citizens of earth,
May we live as the commonwealth of heaven,
For your love's sake.
Amen.[8]

How We See Mary

A great deal of Marian devotion is associated with particular images, through the right brain, the place of images and spatial learning. Likewise, Mary often has been the subject of religious visions. Her appearances usually come to the illiterate and young rather than to learned ecclesiastics. It has been suggested that images of the feminine rise up to balance the rationalistic, literate, and patriarchal predisposition of the culture.[9]

A look at any book of Western art history or a walk through any of the great museums of Europe will show that Mary is the most depicted woman in art. Art is one means to approach Mary, both through appreciating how she has been depicted by others and through one's own artistic expression. Because no physical descriptions were given in the New Testament, early Christian artists first turned to classical imagery and borrowed from ancient images of the Egyptian goddess Isis and her son, Horus. Mary was shown seated, a posture derived from the statuary of rulers, which indicated power. Early European images of Mary, such as the Madonna of Montserrat, the Einsiedeln Madonna, and the Madonna of Rocamadour, show Mary as a powerful queen, in some cases holding a scepter as well as the Christ child. Later in the Middle Ages, the posture changed and Mary was shown standing, and an affectionate, even playful, relationship was portrayed with the child. Great emphasis came to be placed on the familial bonds, and the Holy Family was depicted as an extension of one's own family. In the late medieval period, Mary generally was shown as either a monarch or a peasant. Botticelli depicted Mary as Queen of Heaven crowned in gold, and Raphael showed her as a country woman, with the well-known, rather bored cherubs beneath her. Tender images of Mary and the Christ child from Africa and Asia remind us that the Incarnation comes alive in us when we envision Christ's face as similar to our own.

Sometimes Mary is depicted beside the cross, a grieving figure with a tear-streaked face, the artistic image that most moves Christians. She was probably not as young as Michelangelo's Pietà would have her, but it is likely that she was still in her forties, and given her other children, it is probable she was a grandmother as well. Through Mary at the cross, we see Good Friday in all its pain and sorrow. She is a window, an icon, into comprehending the misery of the cross, and through Jesus' compassion for her, we see through the misery to the mystery of the cross and on to the clear compassion of God.

Not long ago I led a retreat on Mary for a group of Episcopal Church women. Part of the retreat plan was an art project, so we had photocopied a line drawing of an icon of Mary with the Christ child and had many colored pencils available. As the women began to color the icon, conversation slowed and finally stopped, but there was a great deal of energy in the room. For the rest of the allotted time, the group worked in peaceful intensity. When everyone had finished, we gathered the pictures and taped them onto a wall. Each was different from the others, and each one was beautiful. We were all amazed at the work we had produced. It was interesting that few of them had dressed Mary in blue, the color usually associated with Mary (which became fashionable in the twelfth century, when generous patrons allowed artists to work with ground lapis lazuli.)[10] We had shown Mary in reds and purples, greens and golds.

Seeing Mary anew can enrich our theology. While many Christian churches and homes have images of the cross, there is theological justification for images of Mary and the Christ child as well. A seminary professor once spoke to his students about iconography in the church, saying, "Unless somewhere in that church there is . . . some portrayal of Jesus as a baby in his mother's arms, you won't have the whole thing: you won't have the full picture of Christ."[11] The full picture includes Jesus as part of the human family, which includes his mother. Mary speaks not only of the Incarnation, of God becoming enfleshed and being born through us. She speaks also of nurture and tenderness, and shows clearly that human love has a significant role in the expression of God's love among us.

ICONS OF MARY

The first Christian art in the catacombs, though heavily and necessarily symbolic, showed a conscious search for spiritual values, which was apparent in the style used for faces. Like funereal art, it depicted large, open eyes in a face in full communion with God. With Constantine's edict making Christianity the official state religion, art began to reflect God's omnipotence. Constantinople became the center of this new art, combining Christian, Hellenistic, and Oriental influences. Gradually the sacred image found a definitive form.[12]

Following the fifth-century Council of Ephesus, in which Mary was declared Theotokos, Mother of God, a distinct portraiture of Mary began to evolve. The development of the icon in pictorial art, which is considered less a painting than an encounter, paralleled the journey of the faithful as they moved from understanding Mary as a historical personage to viewing her as an intercessor and a spiritual aide. In the eighth century, icons came under heavy attack, but an equally strong defender, John of Damascus, came to their defense, saying, "I do not worship matter; I worship the Creator of matter who became matter for my sake, who willed to take His abode in matter; who worked out my salvation through matter."[13]

In response, in 787,the Second Council of Nicaea made a clear distinction between Jesus, Mary, and the saints. They decided that *latria* is the worship that is given to God alone, *dulia* is the veneration given the saints, and *hyperdulia* is the greater veneration due to Mary as the Mother of God. Consequently veneration of icons was permissible because the veneration went on through the painting to the saint who was represented.

Unlike Western religious art, which often reflects the changing influences of secular art, icon styles have changed little over the centuries. The devotional use of icons is also different from Western Christianity's understanding of art. An icon is meant to open a new process of perception. Its purpose is not to delight the eye but to inform the soul. Icons are similar to the meditation, or *lectio divina,* needed to fully appreciate a passage of scripture. They take time. The stylization of the icon is part of the means by which the grace of the one depicted is transmitted to the viewer. Icons are spiritually interactive and meant to be theology, which is why an artist speaks of "writing" rather than painting an icon. One iconographer wrote: "The image is diagrammatic as well as representational, floating on a sea of philosophy, theology, and mathematics. Folds in the garments converge and spiral into power points; hair curls and waves with the saint's energies; and increasingly bright layers of highlights symbolize levels of consciousness. Light comes primarily from within the figure."[14]

Meditating on icons can help us understand the saints depicted as well as particular passages of scripture. One case in point is a passage in the Second Letter to the Corinthians, where Paul speaks of the gospel, saying "We have this treasure in clay jars."[15] Though Paul is speaking of evangelists who metaphorically carry the treasure of God, Mary literally carried the treasure of God. She is the prototype of all ministers of the gospel, who bear in their bodies the good news of God in Christ. Mary is clearly depicted in one iconographic image as a clay jar. It shows her with her arms lifted in the position of prayer, called the *orans* position, the same position a priest takes while celebrating the Eucharist, and which, interestingly, originated in secular art and was a supplicating pose generally given by young women toward their parents. This icon shows a circle on Mary's body like a large medallion, which is also a window, and there inside is the Christ child. It illustrates Mary both as the source of the Incarnation and as the symbol of the Holy Mother Church. This image is known as the "Theotokos of the Sign," and dates back to the fourth century. It reflects the prophecy of Isaiah 7:14: "Therefore the Lord himself will give you a sign. Look, the young woman is with child and shall bear a son, and shall name him Immanuel." This icon is also sometimes referred to as the Great Panaglía. *Panaglía* means "all holy," and it is a title the Eastern Church has used for Mary since the third century.[16]

Part of the mystical understanding of icons is that the ongoing life of Christ breaks through the temporal in the image and reveals the eternity of God. In the eternity of God, the child is always mystically present in Mary's womb, always taking flesh from her. The icon suggests that as Mary contains the Christ, so do each of us. Saint Francis wrote, "We are His mothers, when we conceive Him in our hearts and bodies by pure love and a clean conscience, and when we bring Him forth by our holy actions, which are to give light and example to others."[17] A Methodist writer, Gordon S. Wakefield, wrote: "Mariology is derived from her part in the Incarnation. She is no goddess, 'merely a woman,' yet it is through her that we live our regenerated lives. She is the mother, in whose embraces the little Christ in us may grow."[18]

The *orans* position of the Great Panaglía clearly connects Mary to the Eucharist. Other artists have done so as well. In the Louvre, in Paris, is an astonishing medieval painting. It is not an icon, yet its unusual image has some components of iconography. It shows Mary as a priest wearing vestments and presiding at the Eucharist. Dated 1438, it was commissioned for the cathedral of Amiens. To contemporary eyes the painting might suggest a medieval enthusiasm of the ordination of women, but it probably spoke more clearly of the Incarnation and its connection to the Eucharist. Clearly, devotion to Mary down the ages did not overlook her connection, through Christ, to the great sacrament of the Christian community.

A contemporary litany makes that clear. It gives thanks for women of faith through the ages, including:

> Saint Elizabeth of Judea, who recognized the value of another
> woman. . .
> Saint Mary Magdalene, minister of Jesus, first evangelist of the
> Christ. . .
> Saint Julian of Norwich, who proclaimed for all of us the moth
> erhood of God. . .

and concludes with Mary,

> Who heard the call of God and answered. . .
> Who drew strength from the woman Elizabeth. . .
> Who turned the Spirit of God into the body and blood of Christ. . .[19]

Through Mary and Holy Spirit, eternal god was transformed into the Christ child, just as the mature Jesus would later transform simple bread and wine into his mystical body in the Eucharist. Sacramental theology begins with the simple statement from the catechism that sacraments are "outward and visible signs of inward and spiritual grace."[20] The sacraments teach us the holiness of the created world, and show that it is through the matter of this world that we receive God's blessings. While John the Baptist's actions initiated the sacrament of Baptism, and through Jesus we have been given the Holy Eucharist, Mary's participation in the Annunciation was the first New Testament event in which God's Spirit was translated into matter.

A rarer iconic composition called "Life-bearing Font," or "Mystical Fountain," originated in Constantinople following a fifth-

century miracle. It shows Mary holding the Christ child and standing in a fountain. The roots of the icon may be in the prophet
Zechariah, where it is written, "On that day a fountain shall be
opened for the house of David and the inhabitants of Jerusalem, to
cleanse them from sin and impurity."[21] The font is shaped like a
chalice. Its image is both baptismal and eucharistic. Just as Mary
encouraged the turning of water into wine at Cana, so, through
bearing Christ into the world, she also made possible the turning of
wine into the Blood of Christ.[22] At the pool surrounding the fountain, people from all walks of life come for healing. In the fountain
image, we glimpse the story of salvation in which Mary continues
to generate the Christ, who in turn is the source of our healing.

While many icons depict Mary as Theotokos, or God-bearer,
devotion to her is essentially devotion to Christ.[23] Her significance
is always in her relationship to the Christ child. Unlike Western images of the Madonna, an icon is not intended to represent tender
maternal love. Rather, the image of the mother holding the Christ
child or with him enthroned on her knees is a symbol of the Incarnation, of God taking human flesh, the central doctrine of the
Christian faith. In an icon the face of the Virgin is one of great se-
riousness. She does not smile but sits with her hair covered by her
veil, or maphorion, and looks down or at the viewer who has come
to adore the child.

MARY AS SPIRITUAL GUIDE

Mary's story and witness are a great source of nourishment for the
faithful. It is up to the seeker to begin to discover the many avenues
of exploration. Although Christians may continue to dwell in either extreme of Marian awareness, there is a middle ground—a via
media—which has been the hallmark of the Anglican tradition in
other theological dilemmas. That way allows us to understand Mary
as a model, a pattern, a paradigm, and as such, a soul friend for us
as we proceed toward the perfection that is Christ. Perhaps it was
necessary for the Church's concept of Mary to become fragmented
and partially eclipsed so that the contemporary Anglican tradition
could find new ways to value the feminine explicitly. However, it is
clearly time for the Anglican tradition to acknowledge Mary as both

a complex biblical figure and a multidimensional archetypal image that have been a source of both inspiration and spiritual nurture.

Reflecting on the life of Mary, with all its joys and sorrows, has been a teaching tool for living down the centuries. Mary's joy was to serve God and to be the means of God's work in the world. She had to work to return again and again to that state of pure joy in which she joined her own will to that of God. She had to recapture the innocence with which she first met God, and be willing to grow in ways she had never imagined. She had been given an opportunity to be a cocreator with God in the Incarnation, and she was challenged again and again to view and love the world as God does. Jesus said that he had come that his joy might be in us and that our joy might be full. He challenged Mary to find joy beyond conventional motherhood and the expectations of this world, yet he understood something of her natural joys. He said in the Gospel of John: "When a women is in labor, she has pain, because her hour has come. But when her child is born, she no longer remembers the anguish because of the joy of having brought a human being into the world."[24] Mary's greatest and most surprising joy came on the other side of the cross.

Likewise Mary suffered sorrows that transcended the personal. Prior to the cross, in following her son, she had learned to swallow her personal pride, which is essential to true humility. The natural human longing for prestige had to give way to a larger vision, and her suffering had to reach beyond personal disappointment, rage, guilt, grief, and depression to embrace the suffering of the whole human family, and to see that family as her own. When Simeon spoke to Mary in the temple and said, "This child is destined for the falling and rising of many in Israel, and to be a sign that will be opposed so that the inner thoughts of many will be revealed—and a sword will pierce your own soul too,"[25] he touched on the inner work that lay ahead for her.

For some, Mary has been held up as an ideal woman. But the ideal woman, as the ideal man, is the one who lives fully the unique personhood God has given to her or him. Mary answered God's call to live out her unique vocation, and people throughout history have learned from her example. In her response to God, "Let it be with me according to your word," she exemplifies the great virtue of humility. It is part of our growth in faith to learn to accept and assent to the will of God. Many demand, "Let it be with me according to my word," and history is strewn with the disordered lives and loves of those who insisted on their own way.

Mary's story continues to nurture people of faith in every age. Her influence continues in our midst, even two thousand years after she lived. She energizes our perception of culture, politics, and social and economic justice. She enriches our understanding of parenting. She invites us to our place at the table with those who have gone before. She demonstrates what can be made of the raw material of each of our lives. A new generation surrounds her now and draws strength from her example. Someday one of those reading these pages, or her or his spouse, child, parent, or friend may find in Mary the needed strength and direction to carry them where they need to go. However we name her—Mother of God, the Blessed Mother, Theotokos, the Virgin Mary, or just Mary—she gives her strong and hard-won testimony to these times, and proves, as ever, to be a faithful guide to the incarnate God.

QUESTIONS FOR STUDY, PRAYER, AND REFLECTION

1. Why do you think a place that is reputed to be a home of Mary has such appeal? What attributes would Mary bring to your home if you invited her to do so? If you could go on a pilgrimage to a place associated with Mary, where would you go?

2. Do you have a favorite image of Mary? Why is it your favorite? Do you have it in a place where you can reflect or meditate on it?

3. Some gardeners have created a garden of flowers named for Mary. Is there a way you could make a sacred space in your garden? What flowers or plants would you have there?

4. How does reflecting on Mary's life help you to identify with women who have suffered? How might you express your concern and make their cause your own?

5. The prophet Micah says that God asks us to "Do justice, and to love kindness, and to walk humbly with your God." Where is pride a danger in your life?

8 💜 Conclusion

"Blessed are you among women, and blessed is the fruit of
your womb." (Luke 1:42)

TENEBRAE

The young man from Tennessee
tells of Tenebrae in his hometown church;
how after the Passion has been read and
candles singularly snuffed, the pastor would
rip a piece of muslin, the severing and
harrowing sound dismissing them
into the dark.

Across the Atlantic, off the Adriatic,
in the water-lapped stones of Cathedral San Marcos,
a side chapel holds a mosaic of Mary. She is
Mater Dolorosa, sitting with her eyes cast down.
But she is working, her hands are busy; she is
sewing the torn curtain, turning the seam
of the frayed fabric—linen legend said she'd woven—
binding the ripped edge of scarlet,
restoring the temple, repairing the breach.

O self and others, slow to forgive,
don't you see? See at last?
Can't you finally understand
how little is required of us?

In the Proevangelium of James, the Annunciation occurred while Mary was weaving the purple and scarlet cloth for the temple curtain, and it was the same curtain that was torn at the moment Christ died. It is a rich image, having the temple curtain made at the time of the announcement of Christ's conception, and torn at the moment of his death. Likewise, it is poignant when the Feast of the Annunciation, which occurs on March 25, coincides with Good Friday. There is an ancient spiritual tradition that the actual Crucifixion occurred on March 25, and poets such as John Donne have honored that intense juxtaposition in verse. We have a human longing for completion, to round out our understanding of Mary's experience and to find a harmonious chord to summarize her life. But her life, like any life except possibly our own, will ultimately elude us. It is for us to continue to ponder her, to follow her, and to learn from her. Nevertheless, our journey through the many roles she had in life has given us some windows to help us better understand Mary for ourselves and for our times.

We have seen Mary emerge as a prophetic voice of the Gospel, one who bore God's Word both in her body and in her proclamation. She rose above her precarious social circumstances, stood tall when the world would reject or dismiss her, and boldly proclaimed that her identity was rooted solely in God. We also have come to see her as the mother of Christ's physical body and of Christ's mystical body, which includes all Christians. We see some of the seeds of his teaching in her words. In addition, we have come to understand her as a woman who embodied the fullness of life as shown by her fruitful marriage and active family life. Furthermore, we have seen her as the first Christian theologian, cultivating the thinking that is centered in the emotive and moral spheres and culminating in intellectual sincerity, a union of mind and heart. We have followed her as a disciple, as she traveled the difficult road that led to the cross and bore the suffering that came of her unique circumstances.

We understood that she was one who consoled and was consoled by the incarnate God, and as such can offer consolation to us who are now trying to serve the world as Christians. And finally, we perceived her as a paradigm of faith, her life a pattern to emulate both in the acceptance of inevitable suffering and in the celebration of equally inevitable joy.

Not long ago I mentioned to a Roman Catholic woman that I was writing about Mary. As we discussed Mary and she shared her enthusiasm for the study of Mary, she suddenly stopped and asked, "If you are interested in Mary, why don't you become a Roman Catholic?" Clearly she thought that Mary was somehow more a part of the Roman Catholic tradition and, in a sense, was more accessible through that branch of Christianity. I disagree with that assumption, and hope the previous chapters have demonstrated that Mary is indeed a part of the Anglican tradition and that knowledge of our roots draws us closer to her. Though the Roman Catholic Church kept an active Mariology alive following the Reformation, the changes of Vatican II did much to remove Mary from the church's mainstream for subsequent generations. But tremendous interest and energy still remain for Roman Catholics around the person of Mary, in part because she represents the feminine for a tradition in which women do not exercise full and equal leadership. Although the Anglican Communion is significantly smaller than our Roman counterpart, our church's history has exposed Marian devotion to a full range of new and liberating possibilities for women, which will be useful in predicting the future of Mariology for churches yet to realize women's pastoral and liturgical potential.

I believe that a reassessment of Mary has much to offer the contemporary church, both to individuals in their prayer lives and to the life of the institutional church. In addition to a greater appreciation of the dimensions and richness of Mary's life and what her life teaches us, the church also stands to receive three significant gifts:

The first gift is a window into the love of God, and Mary not only aids our understanding of God's love for us but also shows how one individual woman loved God. We know that Mary influenced her son and that Jesus taught with several images of the feminine divine. In the actual life of Mary, as glimpsed in the gospels, we have the figure of a parent who doggedly followed her child despite the cost, a figure whose love was comparable to that shown by the father of the prodigal son in Jesus' parable (Luke 15:11-24). For those individuals whose experiences with their own fathers offer less of a window to God than do the experiences with their mothers, a focus on the life of Mary gives another parable on parental love and connects positive experiences of maternal love with the faithful love of God.

The second gift that a reassessment of Mary offers is a reminder of the valuable participation of women, past and present. Images of the Madonna and Child speak to us of the Incarnation as nothing else does. But they also speak to us of a woman's participation, her assent to give the miracle life. Images of Mary remind us of the gifts and participation of women that have often been neglected, and they show us a picture of one made in the image of God who bore and birthed God among us. Though we now have female clergy and women in positions of lay leadership, it is important to remember the centuries of traditional volunteer labor that women have given to the church, as members of altar guilds, as makers of vestments, as those who cook and clean to offer hospitality in Christ's name.

The third gift that a reassessment of Mary brings is to locate us back into our humanity and into this world with which we have been entrusted. Mary reminds us of the flesh, the human, the frail and yielding body that is each of us. As a woman who gave birth in a stable, she calls us back to the simple values of caring for this world with its plants and animals. As a poor woman, she reminds us that the real treasures of Earth are our living, breathing selves and those we love, and this magnificent creation of which we are privileged briefly to be a part. We are now aware that Earth's ecological balance is in serious danger. To love the created world is to love the Creator, and Mary reminds us of our creatureliness. Like each of us, Mary was born into a particular time and place, and given fleeting, precious hours that fly quickly beyond reach. Her humanity reminds us to treasure and preserve this astonishing and beautiful creation—each unique and bright particularity—for our children and for those yet to be, so that we, like her, may be called a blessing by all generations.

Notes

NOTES TO CHAPTER 2: AS PROPHET

1. *The Interpreter's Dictionary of the Bible,* ed. George A. Buttrick, vol. 3 (Nashville: Abingdon Press, 1962), s.v. "prophet," 897.
2. Galatians 4:4.
3. Luke 1:26–38.
4. Raymond E. Brown, *The Birth of the Messiah: A Commentary on the Infancy Narratives in the Gospels of Matthew and Luke* (New York: Doubleday, 1993), 290.
5. Gail McMurray Gibson, *The Theater of Devotion: East Anglian Drama and Society in the Late Middle Ages* (Chicago: University of Chicago Press, 1989), fig. 6.5.
6. Walter Wangerin Jr., "The Christ Mass" ("Antistrophe"), in *The Manger Is Empty* (San Francisco: Harper and Row, 1989), 55.
7. John MacQuarrie, *Mary for All Christians* (Edinburgh: T & T Clark, Ltd., 1990), 3–4.
8. Hans Küng, *On Being a Christian,* trans. Edward Quinn (Garden City, NY: Doubleday, 1976), 457.
9. John 3:1–10.
10. Jean Shinoda Bolen, *Goddesses in Every Woman* (New York: Harper and Row, 1984), 35–36.
11. Norman Pittenger, *Our Lady: The Mother of Jesus in Christian Faith and Devotion* (London: SCM Press, 1996), 75.
12. Frank Griswold, "Some Reflections on Sexuality," from "Not Ourselves: For the Clergy of the Episcopal Church from the Presiding Bishop," autumn 1999.
13. Luke 1:39–45.
14. Judges 5:24.
15. Marina Warner, *Alone of All Her Sex: The Myth and Cult of the Virgin Mary* (New York: Vintage Books, 1976), 12.
16. 1 Samuel 2:1–10.
17. Judith 15:12–16:17.
18. Exodus 15:20–21.
19. Luke 1:46–55.
20. Walter Brueggemann, *The Prophetic Imagination* (Philadelphia: Fortress, 1978), 13.
21. Martin Luther, "The Magnificat," in *Luther's Works,* vol. 21 (St. Louis: Concordia, 1956), 306.
22. Genesis 12:2.
23. Rubem A. Alves, *The Poet, the Warrior, the Prophet* (Philadelphia: Trinity Press International, 1990), 137.
24. Exodus 15:20.

25. *A Commentary on Pseudo-Philo's Liber Antiquitatum Biblicarum,* vol. 1, trans. H. Jacobson (Leiden: Brill, 1996), 105. Quoted in Richard Bauckham, *Gospel Women: Studies of the Named Women in the Gospels* (Grand Rapids, MI: Eerdmans, 2002), 271–272.
26. 2 Kings 22:14–20.
27. Judges 5:28–31.
28. 1 Samuel 2:1.
29. Nick Aiken and Rowan Williams, *Family Prayers* (Mahwah, NJ: Paulist Press, 2002), 26.
30. Luke 6:36.
31. Matthew 5:7.
32. Matthew 18:33.
33. Matthew 9:13.
34. Amos 8:6.
35. Luke 4:18.
36. Luke 6:20,24.
37. Matthew 10:9–13.
38. Luke 11:3.
39. Micah 6:8.
40. Matthew 11:29.
41. Luke 14:11.
42. Luke 2:36–38.
43. Bauckham, *Gospel Women,* 99.
44. *The Hymnal 1982* (New York: Church Hymnal Corp.: 1982), 664.
45. Acts 21:9.
46. John 2:1–11.
47. Mark 6:3.
48. Genesis 41:55.

NOTES TO CHAPTER 3: AS MATRIARCH
1. Genesis 3:6, emphasis added.
2. Genesis18:14.
3. Luke 1:37.
4. 1 Samuel 2:1–8.
5. Cynthia Ozick, "Hannah and Elkanah: Torah as the Matrix for Feminism," in *Out of the Garden: Women Writers on the Bible,* eds. Christina Büchmann and Celina Spiegel (New York: Fawcett Columbine, 1944), 89.
6. Jaroslav Pelikan, *Mary Through the Centuries: Her Place in the History of Culture* (New Haven, CT: Yale University Press, 1996), 17.
7. Hans Küng, *On Being a Christian,* 450–453.
8. Matthew 1:18–23.
9. Isaiah 7:14.
10. Brown, *The Birth of the Messiah,* 149.
11. Matthew 1:18–25.
12. Ivone Gebara and Maria Clara Bingemer, trans. Phillip Berryman, *Mary: Mother of God, Mother of the Poor* (Maryknoll, NY: Orbis Books, 1987), 48–52.
13. John 4:7–30.
14. Mark 7:24–30.

15. Luke 8:43–48.
16. Luke 7:36–50.
17. Window in Saint Mary's Episcopal Church, Pacific Grove, CA.
18. Alicia Craig Faxon, *Women and Jesus* (Philadelphia: Pilgrim Press, 1973), 24–25.
19. Leviticus 12:1–2, 4–8.
20. Luke 2:22–24.
21. *The Complete Gospels: Annotated Scholars Version,* ed. Robert Miller (Sonoma, CA: Polebridge Press, 1992), 376.
22. Matthew 18:3.
23. Luke 10:21.
24. Lucien Deiss, C.S.Sp., *Joseph, Mary, Jesus,* trans. Madeleine Beaumont (Collegeville, MN: Liturgical Press, 1996), 87.
25. Luke 4:16–20.
26. John 8:1–11.
27. Mark 6:3.
28. Joseph Grassi, *Mary, Mother and Disciple* (Wilmington, DE: Michael Glazier, Inc., 1988), 121.
29. Hilda Graef, *Mary, A History of Doctrine and Devotion,* vol. 1 (New York: Sheed and Ward, 1963), 70.
30. Galatians 3:29.
31. Miller, *Complete Gospels,* 386.
32. Ibid., 387.
33. *Apocrypha Syriaca:The Proevangelium Jacobi and Transitus Mariae,* Studia Sinaitica, no. XI, ed. and trans. Agnes Smith Lewis (London: C. J. Clay and Sons, 1902), 5.
34. Demetra Velasarios Jaquet, "Mary: The Model for Contemplative Life," in *The Living Pulpit,* vol. 10, no. 4, Oct.–Dec. 2001, 18.
35. John 19:25.
36. Graef, *The Devotion to Our Lady* (New York: Hawthorn Books, 1963), 47.
37. Peter and Linda Murray, *The Oxford Companion to Christian Art and Architecture* (Oxford, England: Oxford University Press, 1996), 313.
38. *The HarperCollins Encyclopedia of Catholicism,* gen. ed. Richard P. McBrien (San Francisco: HarperSanFrancisco, 1995), 815.
39. Luigi Gambero, *Mary and the Fathers of the Church* (San Francisco: Ignatius Press, 1999), 157.
40. Ibid., 221.
41. Grassi, *Mary, Mother and Disciple,* 121.
42. Gambero, *Mary and the Fathers,* 65.
43. Matthew 1:18.
44. Matthew 1:24–25.
45. Luke 2:7.
46. John Painter, *Just James: The Brother of Jesus in Scripture and Tradition* (Minneapolis: Fortress Press, 1999), 35.
47. Galatians 1:19.
48. John Sutherland Black, "Mary" in *Encyclopaedia Britannica,* 11th ed., vol. XVII (New York: The Encyclopaedia Britannica Company, 1911), 812.
49. *Book of Common Prayer* (New York: Oxford, 1979), 391.
50. Matthew 22:1–14.

NOTES TO CHAPTER 4: AS THEOLOGIAN

1. *American Heritage Dictionary of the English Language,* ed. William Morris (Boston: American Heritage Publishing Co., Inc., 1969), 1334.
2. Matthew 1:15–16.
3. Matthew 1:21.
4. Brown, *The Birth of the Messiah,* 138–142.
5. R. Travers Herford, *Christianity in Talmud and Midrash* (New York: KTAV Publishing House, Inc., 1975), 48.
6. Genesis 38:9.
7. Genesis 38:25–26.
8. Ann Belford Ulanov, *The Female Ancestors of Christ* (Boston: Shambhala, 1993), 24.
9. Mark 7:24–30.
10. Joshua 2:11.
11. Pamela Berger, *The Goddess Obscured: Transformation of the Grain Protectress from Goddess to Saint* (Boston: Beacon Press, 1985), 90–91.
12. Hebrews 11:31.
13. Matthew 21:31b–32.
14. Bauckham, *Gospel Women,* 2–3.
15. Ruth 1:16.
16. Ruth 1:21.
17. Ruth 4:12.
18. Ruth 4:14–15.
19. Ulanov, *Female Ancestors,* 71.
20. 1 Kings 1:11–27.
21. John 8:41.
22. Jane Schaberg, *The Illegitimacy of Jesus: A Feminist Theological Interpretation of the Infancy Narratives* (San Francisco: Harper and Row, 1987), 170.
23. Ibid., 165.
24. Ibid., 195–199.
25. Herford, *Christianity in Talmud and Midrash,* 40.
26. Galatians 4:4.
27. Brown, *The Birth of the Messiah,* 537–541.
28. Robert Aron, *The Jewish Jesus* (Maryknoll, NY: Orbis Books, 1968), 5.
29. Ibid., 21–25.
30. Luke 2:21.
31. Genesis 17:10–13.
32. Aron, *The Jewish Jesus,* 27.
33. Ibid., 27.
34. Luke 2:29–32.
35. Luke 2:34–35.
36. *American Heritage Dictionary,* 1086.
37. Luke 1:34.
38. Luke 2:48.
39. Timothy Ware, *The Orthodox Church* (Baltimore: Penguin Books,1963), 74.
40. Jelaluddin Rumi, "Two Kinds of Intelligence," in *This Longing: Poetry, Teaching Stories, and Letters of Rumi,* trans. Coleman Barks and John Moyne (Boston and London: Shambhala, 2000), 36.
41. Paul Pearsall, *The Heart's Code: Tapping the Wisdom and Power of the Heart's Energy* (New York: Broadway Books, 1998), 111–112.

42. Marion J. Hatchett, *Commentary on the American Prayer Book* (San Francisco: HarperSanFrancisco, 1979), 395.
43. Luke 2:18–19.
44. Luke 2:51.
45. Beverly Roberts Gaventa, *Mary: Glimpses of the Mother of God* (Minneapolis: Fortress Press, 1995), 130.
46. Patrick D. Miller, "The Church's First Theologian," in *Theology Today,* October 1999, 293–296.
47. Isaiah 42:1–4.
48. Luke 22:27.
49. Matthew 6:10.
50. Pelikan, *Mary Through the Centuries,* 84.
51. Luke 10:38–42.

NOTES TO CHAPTER 5: AS DISCIPLE
1. Luke 6:17.
2. Luke 19:37.
3. Luke 10:1–16.
4. Luke 24:6–7.
5. Luke 9:18.
6. Luke 2:5–7.
7. Matthew 2:11–12.
8. A. N. Wilson, *Jesus: A Life* (New York: W. W. Norton and Co., 1992), 81.
9. Peter Daino, *Mother of Sorrows, Mother of Defiance* (Maryknoll, NY: Orbis Books, 1993). Quoted in *The Living Pulpit,* vol. 10, no. 4, Oct.–Dec. 2001, 31.
10. Matthew 2:13–15
11. Matthew 2:19–21.
12. Deuteronomy 16:16.
13. Luke 2:41–51.
14. Douglas Edwards, *The Virgin Birth in History and Faith* (London: Faber and Faber, Ltd., 1943), 182–184.
15. Miller, "The Church's First Theologian," 378–379.
16. Quoted in Hans Urs Von Balthazar, *The Threefold Garland* (San Francisco: Ignatius Press, 1978), 64.
17. Mark 3:20–21.
18. Mark 3:30–35.
19. Mark 6:2–5.
20. Matthew 10:34–37.
21. Luke 11:27–28.
22. John Painter, *Just James: The Brother of Jesus in History and Tradition* (Minneapolis: Fortress, 1999), 5.
23. Richard Bauckham, *Jude and the Relatives of Jesus in the Early Church* (Edinburgh: T & T Clark, 1990), 233–234.
24. Ibid., 282–288.
25. Dietrich Bonhoeffer, *The Cost of Discipleship* (New York: Macmillan, 1949), 45–60.
26. John 8:1–11.
27. John 19:25–27.
28. John de Satgé, *Mary and the Christian Gospel* (London: SPCK, 1976), 57.
29. Dante Alighieri, "Paradiso," in *The Divine Comedy,* with translation

and comment by John D. Sinclair (New York: Oxford, 1939), 479.
30. Luke 24:18.
31. Bauckham, *Gospel Women,* 208.
32. Sarah Beckwith, *Signifying God: Social Relation and Symbolic Act in the York Corpus Christi Plays* (Chicago: University of Chicago Press, 2001), 72.
33. Unpublished adaptation of the Montecassino Passion Play by Matthew Griffin, 2002.
34. Icon by Tatiana Romanova Grant at Prophet Elias Greek Orthodox Church in Santa Cruz, CA.
35. Livingston Memorial Window, Saint Peter's Episcopal Church, New York, NY.
36. Mark 15:40–41.
37. Mark 15:47–16:1.
38. Mark 6:3.
39. Bauckham, *Gospel Women,* 253.
40. Robert Eisenman, *James the Brother of Jesus* (New York: Penguin,1997),753.
41. Raymond E. Brown, *The Death of the Messiah,* vol. 2 (New York: Doubleday, 1994), 1017.
42. Painter, *Just James,* 34.
43. Matthew 27:56.
44. Matthew 10:3.
45. Matthew 28:1.
46. Eisenman, *James the Brother of Jesus,* xxvii–xxvii.
47. Brown, *The Death of the Messiah,* 226.
48. Bauckham, *Jude and the Relatives of Jesus in the Early Church,* 37–38.
49. Eisenman, *James the Brother of Jesus,* 753.
50. Luke 8:1–3.
51. Luke 24:10.
52. *Pictorial Bible Dictionary,* ed. Merrill C. Tenney (Nashville: Southwestern Company, 1974), 52.
53. 1 Corinthians 9:5.
54. Acts 1:14.
55. *The Hymnal 1982,* 673.

NOTES TO CHAPTER 6: AS INTERCESSOR
1. de Satgé, *Mary and the Christian Gospel,* 82.
2. A. M. Allchin, *The Joy of All Creation: An Anglican Meditation on the Place of Mary* (Cambridge,MA: Cowley, 1984), 108–112.
3. Revelation 12:1–17.
4. Virgil Elizondo, *Guadalupe: Mother of the New Creation* (Maryknoll, NY: Orbis, 1997), 5–22.
5. Michael P. Carroll, *The Cult of the Virgin Mary: Psychological Origins* (Princeton, NJ: Princeton University Press, 1986), 182–194.
6. Elizondo, *Guadalupe,* 8.
7. John 2:5.
8. Carlos Touché Porter, *A Short History of Anglican Worship in Mexico* (unpublished paper, 1996).
9. Allchin, *The Joy of All Creation,* 151–152.
10. Hosea 13:8.
11. Isaiah 42:14.

12. Luke 15:8–10.
13. Mark 12:29.
14. Geoffrey Ashe, *The Virgin* (London: Routledge and Kegan Paul, 1976), 150–153.
15. John 1:1–3.
16. Brown, *The Death of the Messiah,* 140–142.
17. Julian of Norwich, *Showings,* trans. Edmund Colledge, OSA, and James Walsh, SJ (Mahwah, NJ: Paulist Press, 1978), 292.
18. Elizabeth Johnson, *She Who Is: The Mystery of God in Feminist Theological Discourse* (New York: Crossroad Publishing, 1992), 102–103.
19. Gordon Light, "She Comes Sailing on the Wind," *Common Praise: Anglican Church of Canada* (Toronto: Anglican Book Centre, 1998), 656.
20. *Book of Common Prayer,* 359.
21. Shirley du Boulay, *Tutu, Voice of the Voiceless* (Grand Rapids, MI: Eerdmanns, 1988), 74.
22. *Book of Common Prayer,* 857.
23. C. S. Lewis, *Letters to Malcolm: Chiefly on Prayer,* quoted in *Mary is for Everyone: Essays on Mary and Ecumenism* eds. William McLoughlin and Jill Pinnock (Herefordshire, England: Gracewing, 1997), 296.
24. John 2:3.
25. Adapted from Black, "Mary" in *Encyclopaedia Britannica,* 813.
26. *The Hymnal 1982,* 258.
27. Ibid., 618.
28. Mary Clayton, *The Cult of the Virgin Mary in Anglo-Saxon England* (Cambridge, England: Cambridge University Press, 1990), 90–91.
29. Quoted in *A Sourcebook about Mary,* eds. Robert J. Baker and Barbara Budde (Chicago: Liturgy Training Publications, 2002), 116.
30. Beverly Boyd, *The Middle English Miracles of the Virgin* (San Marino, CA: The Huntington Library, 1964), 10.
31. George H. Tavard, *The Thousand Faces of the Virgin Mary* (Collegeville, MN: Liturgical Press, 1996), 134–152.
32. William Forbes, quoted in *The Blessed Virgin Mary: Essays by Anglicans,* eds. E. L. Mascall and H. S. Box (London: Darton, Longman, and Todd, Ltd., 1963), 58.
33. Warner, *Alone of All Her Sex,* 288.
34. Robert Llewellyn, *The Doorway to Silence: The Contemplative Use of the Rosary* (Darton, Longman and Todd, Ltd., 1986), 12.
35. Janet Coles and Robert Budwig, *Beads: An Exploration of Bead Traditions Around the World* (New York: Simon and Schuster, 1997), 8.
36. Warner, *Alone of All Her Sex,* 305.
37. Luke 1:28.
38. Luke 1:42.
39. J. Neville Ward, *Five for Sorrow, Ten for Joy: A Consideration of the Rosary* (Garden City, NY: Doubleday, 1973).
40. Thomas Schultz, *The Rosary for Episcopalians* (Berkeley, CA: Incarnation Priory, 1992), 7.
41. From a conversation with the Rev. Leilani Nelson, Sept. 4, 2001.
42. Allchin, *The Joy of All Creation,* 145–146.
43. From the Order of Service for the Solemn Mass of the Church of Saint Mary the Virgin, 145 West 46th Street, New York, NY.

NOTES TO CHAPTER 7: AS PARADIGM

1. Vincenzina Krymow, *Mary's Flowers: Gardens, Legends, and Meditations* (Cincinnati, OH: St. Anthony Messenger Press, 1999), 160–173.
2. Martin Stevens, *Four Middle English Mystery Cycles* (Princeton, NJ: Princeton University Press, 1987), 197.
3. Mary Clayton, *The Cult of the Virgin Mary in Anglo-Saxon England* (Cambridge, England: Cambridge University Press, 1990), 139–140.
4. Ibid., 140.
5. Margaret Gallyon, *Margery Kempe of Lynn and Medieval England* (Norwich, England: Canterbury Press, 1995), 19.
6. Robert McAfee Brown, *Theology in a New Key: Responding to Liberation Theology* (Philadelphia: Westminster Press, 1978), 100.
7. *A Sourcebook about Mary*, eds. J. Robert Baker and Barbara Budde (Chicago: Liturgy Training Publications: 2002), 100.
8. Stuart Thomas, quoted in "New Life Within Us: A Service for Lady Day 2000," a publication of The Mother's Union, Mary Summer House, 24 Tufton Street, London SW1P3RB. Note: the congregational responses were omitted.
9. Leonard Shlain, *The Alphabet Versus the Goddess: The Conflict Between Word and Image* (Arkana, NY: Penguin 1998), 265–266.
10. Michel Pastoureau, *Blue: The History of a Color* (Princeton: NJ: Princeton University Press, 2001), 49–55.
11. Pittenger, *Our Lady,* 73.
12. Egon Sendler, *The Icon: Image of the Invisible, Elements of Theology, Aesthetics and Technique,* trans. Steven Bigham (Torrance, CA: Oakwood Publications, 1988), 14–15.
13. Quoted in Sendler, *The Icon,* 40.
14. Betsy Porter, "Byzantine-style Icons," an article from the World Wide Web: *www.saintgregorys.org.*
15. 2 Corinthians 4:7.
16. Gambero, *Mary and the Fathers of the Church,* 77.
17. Saint Francis of Assisi, *His Life and Writings,* trans. Leo Sherley-Price (London: A. R. Mowbray and Sons, 1959), 184.
18. Gordon S. Wakefield, "The Blessed Virgin Mary in some modern poets," in *Mary is for Everyone,* 299.
19. Joan Chittister, "A Litany of Women in the Church," quoted in Elizabeth Johnson, *Friends of God and Prophets: A Feminist Theological Reading of the Communion of Saints* (New York: Continuum, 1998), 257.
20. *Book of Common Prayer,* 857.
21. Zechariah 13:1.
22. From an e-mail correspondence with the Rev. Steve Wilson, March 5, 2002.
23. Michael P. Carroll, *The Cult of the Virgin Mary: Psychological Origins* (Princeton, NJ: Princeton University Press, 1986), 20.
24. John 16:21.
25. Luke 2:34–35.